VGM Careers for You Series

CAREERS FOR
CARING
PEOPLE
& Other Sensitive Types

ADRIAN PARADIS
Revised by Luisa Gerasimo

SECOND EDITI

D1304724

VGM Career Books

Chicago New York San Francisco Lisbon London Madrid Mexico City
Milan New Delhi San Juan Seoul Singapore Sydney Toronto

The McGraw·Hill Companies

Library of Congress Cataloging-in-Publication Data

Paradis, Adrian A.
Careers for caring people & other sensitive types / Adrian Paradis.— 2nd ed.
p. cm. — (Careers for you series)
Includes bibliographical references.
ISBN 0-07-140572-0 (pbk.)
1. Human services—Vocational guidance—United States. 2. Social service—
Vocational guidance—United States. 3. Medical care—Vocational guidance—United
States. 4. Child care services—Vocational guidance—United States. I. Title:
Careers for caring people and other sensitive types. II. Title. III. VGM careers
for you series.

HV10.5.p368 2003
362′.023—dc21

2002192403

2 3 4 5 6 7 8 9 0   LBM/LBM   2 1 0 9 8 7 6 5 4 3

ISBN 0-07-140572-0

McGraw-Hill books are available at special quantity discounts to use as premiums and
sales promotions, or for use in corporate training programs. For more information, please
write to the Director of Special Sales, Professional Publishing, McGraw-Hill, Two Penn
Plaza, New York, NY 10121-2298. Or contact your local bookstore.

This book is printed on acid-free paper.

Contents

CHAPTER ONE

The Call to Caregiving

For many of us, the tragic events of September 11, 2001, changed everything. Those whose lives were directly touched by the loss of a loved one, a job, or a place to live were forced to rethink their goals and their lives. For the millions of us who watched the events in stunned horror from the safety of our homes that morning, the need to rethink things was gentler and yet, for many, no less insistent. We suddenly were reminded that there is no guarantee of tomorrow. As the shock was barely wearing off, millions of Americans from every walk of life responded to the events of September 11th by focusing on giving. The world has seldom seen a faster or larger response to a human disaster. People showed they cared. People gave. People responded.

In the welling up of emotion that is natural after a shocking disaster, many people looked at their current jobs and said, "Not good enough." Watching the heroic New York Fire Department and other first responders made many folks realize that life has more meaning when you are involved in helping others. Many people said to themselves that the time had come to consider new paths, and perhaps new careers.

In those terrible weeks of recovery, something interesting happened in our nation. Truck drivers entered school to become teachers. Retired executives came out of retirement to create and run new charitable organizations. Stockbrokers switched to teaching high school. Moms and dads decided to spend more time with their children and to tell them out loud how much they are loved. There are probably thousands of examples of people who made large and small changes in the ensuing months. For many people, and perhaps for you, a life spent caring for others is the kind of life that is filled with meaning.

An Overview of Caregiving

Each morning, noon, and night, thousands of caregivers—both men and women—experience a warm welcome as they arrive to start their shifts, watching over or caring for the sick, the disturbed, the lonely, and the elderly, or the very young, all of whom require caregivers. At the end of the shift, their places are taken by other caregivers—a never-ending cycle that calls for untold numbers of dedicated workers.

The caregiver—whether in the home, the hospital, nursing home, a home health agency, or a rescue squad—has become one of the most important people in the health field. Thousands of families could not properly care for a sick family member were it not for the therapist, aide, or nurse who comes daily to provide care. Hospitals need aides to perform countless duties, many formerly performed by the professional nursing staff, now assigned more administrative duties. Nursing homes depend on the nurses and aides who provide the care their residents require.

There are countless others who have equally important responsibilities as they care for children, elderly people, and others who need help. For example, social service workers daily shoulder the often heartbreaking tasks of helping broken families and tormented individuals, trying to solve myriad problems.

As you read, you may be surprised to discover many avenues open to those who seek a career in some aspect of caregiving. For example, the "support staff"—the men and women who provide office services—are essential to the operation of every hospital, nursing home, and other caregiving agency. They hold titles such as administrator, receptionist, computer operator, accountant, public relations manager, and file clerk. In hospitals and other institutions, essential employees include not only the office staff, but also those who work as housekeepers, custodians, maintenance specialists, cafeteria workers, porters, and other nonmedical personnel.

The primary focus of this book is positions that call for briefer training periods, more practical for those with limited financial resources who need to start earning as soon as possible. This book excludes coverage of members of the professional medical corps such as doctors, dentists, and specialists who are so vital to our health care system.

You can, however, obtain information about these professions in some of the books listed in Appendix A. Data on the total number of workers, earnings, employment outlook, and minimum years of training required for medical professionals as well as other caregivers are presented in Appendix B.

Personal Qualifications

Because caregiving includes so many different kinds of jobs, there is probably a place for you, regardless of your mental or physical abilities, interests, or personality.

Personal qualifications for nonprofessional positions are not usually difficult to meet. The position you choose should be yours if you display an interest in learning, a sense of responsibility, and willingness to work hard and bring to the job the skills required.

But if you are looking forward to a career as a registered nurse, licensed practical nurse, certified nurse's aide, therapist, emergency medical technician, or other paramedical job, the requirements can be quite demanding:

- Good physical health and emotional strength. These are of first importance to enable you to tolerate the long, irregular hours and bear the general strain of being available during times of emergency.

- Reliability and a sense of responsibility. The lives of others may be in your hands on occasion. The willingness with which you use those hands, and the care and conscientiousness with which you direct them, will play an important part in recovery, recuperation, and a return to satisfying life for many you have not yet met.
- Eagerness to learn and willingness to study hard. Modern medical skills and techniques require application to books, computers, laboratory work, lectures, and each aspect of the training program.
- Intellectual curiosity, the kind that makes it difficult for you to leave an unsolved problem or walk away from an unanswered question, is a lifetime "must," not only during your years of education, but throughout your professional life.
- A genuine liking for people, an understanding of their fears and needs, must be developed and strengthened throughout your career, for you will deal with people who want and need your personal as well as your professional best.
- Humor, tolerance, discretion, and a giving nature are the other attributes you should have.

Every profession has certain drawbacks, and caregiving is no exception. There are not many opportunities to make a fortune, although salaries have improved and continue to rise. Chances for advancement are also good. The work may be harder and the hours longer than in another occupation. You may be exposed to much pain and suffering, mental disturbance, and human travail and sorrow. You may be required to take long and expensive training. You will be expected to demonstrate an unselfishness that places job before self-interest.

Job Availability

No matter where you live, you will find caregivers working in hospitals, medical offices, homes, child- and senior-care facilities, or in organizations dedicated to helping the young, elderly, indigent, sick, mentally disturbed, and those suffering from substance abuse and other problems. As the population grows, and the number of seniors continues to increase, the need to provide elder care will become especially urgent.

Those who live in rural areas may have to travel a distance to work. Unlike some fields, such as transportation, manufacturing, or tourism, where jobs are concentrated in definite places, opportunities for caregivers are found wherever people live.

Because so much of this book is devoted to opportunities in the health field, projected employment growth information from the United States Department of Labor Web page is included here:

"Wage and salary employment in the health services industry is projected to increase more than 25 percent through 2010, compared with an average of 16 percent for all industries.... Employment growth is expected to account for 2.8 million new jobs—13 percent of all wage and salary jobs added to the economy over the 2000–2010 period. Projected rates of employment growth for the various segments of this industry range from 10 percent in hospitals, the largest and slowest growing industry segment, to 68 percent in the much smaller home health care services."

Rewards

Here are some of the rewards you will find as a caregiver:

- Training, whether it is for a CNA (Certified Nursing Assistant) or for a brain surgeon, will bring you a measure of prestige.

- Job stability helps make up for lower salaries.
- Working conditions are usually good.
- Institutions and agencies are becoming more generous with fringe benefits.
- People dedicated to their professions make pleasant associates. You will experience a genuine sense of partnership with others in your work.
- Doing a worthwhile job brings true personal satisfaction.

No matter what your caregiving position may be, you will feel a certain pride in your work. You will feel pride in providing an essential, sometimes life-preserving service and pride in being part of a nationwide body of men and women who are helping humanity, whether you are the surgeon, nurse, aide, nanny, social worker, or even the receptionist or computer operator. It takes all kinds of caregivers to provide the care the world needs.

CHAPTER TWO

The Path to Caregiving

I f you are drawn to the idea of caring for others in some capacity but hesitate to investigate the field because you are uncomfortable about your age or have limited education or no money to pay for schooling, this chapter should encourage you to pursue your career search.

Age Is No Barrier

You can be twelve years old serving as a baby-sitter or eighty and working as a companion. Age is no barrier for caretakers. Although the majority of caregivers probably start their careers right after completing high school, college, or graduate school, it is never too late to join the army of concerned men and women who serve those in need of health, personal, or other kinds of care. It is not uncommon to make a mid-career shift and find employment in an entirely different field, to join the workforce after raising children and managing a home, or to spend retirement years in a new field. In fact, it has been estimated that over a lifetime, many people hold between eight and twelve different jobs. Therefore, no matter what your age, you can find new purpose in your life—just like Hilda Swenson and Roderick Hector.

When Hilda Swenson turned forty, she made two decisions: she would leave the frigid Minnesota winters and trade her tiresome accounting job for something that would help humanity. She had done her share of volunteer work, but now she wanted to become a caring nurse. Aware that in some areas there was no need for additional nurses, she knew she would need to do some research before relocating. When she vacationed in Florida, she visited a number of hospitals, nursing homes, and life-care establishments and decided that she could find employment once she obtained the necessary training. A year later, she had her LPN certificate and fulfilled her goal.

Similarly, Roderick Hector, a high school coach, realized that with the school budget crunch in California, it would be only a matter of time before he lost his job. Like Hilda, he wanted to work with people in a health setting and decided to become a physical therapist, another occupation that called for only a year in graduate school since he already had a bachelor's degree.

Hilda and Roderick are examples of how those approaching midlife can switch occupations and pursue a far more satisfying career—with proper preparation!

Jobs for All Levels of Training

Without a high school diploma, you face the greatest difficulty finding a job. Low-paying positions, such as kitchen work in institutions, custodian positions, inside or outside maintenance jobs, or hospital porter assignments, lifting patients or moving heavy objects, are probably the most common jobs in the field of caretaking for those seeking work without a high school education. If you find yourself needing that high school diploma, contact the guidance counseling office at your high school or vocational-technical school. The staff there can direct you to the resources you need to obtain a high school diploma or a G.E.D. (general equivalency diploma).

On the other hand, if you have a high school diploma, you should find many more job openings, especially if you have acquired some useful skill. As you progress up the educational ladder to a certificate from a vocational-technical school or community college, you have tangible skills to offer and become eligible for better-paying jobs. Some of the caregiving vocational-technical skills you can learn in two years or less include:

- Dental assistant
- Dental receptionist
- Dietetic technician
- Doctor's assistant
- Emergency medical technician (EMT)
- Food-service specialist
- Inhalation therapy technician
- Medical assistant
- Medical/dental receptionist
- Medical laboratory technician
- Medical office manager
- Medical secretary
- Nurse's aide
- Operating-room technician
- Orderly
- Practical nurse
- Vocational nurse

A college diploma elevates one into another world where responsibilities and earnings, as well as the breadth of job opportunities, are much greater.

No Experience Needed for Entry-Level Jobs

Joyce Kabien had served as a candy striper in a nearby hospital during high school. Although her assignments were usually of a routine unskilled nature—delivering mail, operating the book cart, escorting patients to physical therapy, serving between-meal snacks—she had learned enough about how a hospital operates to know that she would find satisfaction working there after high school. Because of her volunteer service, the administrator gladly gave her an entry-level job in the cafeteria, which enabled Joyce to attend night school to train as a Certified Nurse's Aide (CNA). After she worked in this position for a time, she returned to school to take the necessary courses to become a Licensed Practical Nurse (LPN).

Similarly, Warren Emmons worked after school and during vacations for a nursing home. He cut grass, trimmed, raked, and picked up trash. Once out of high school, the home employed him as a full-time custodian, enabling him to continue his education at a community college to prepare for an all-around maintenance job. He soon took the place of the retiring maintenance director.

Although volunteer service during high school is not a necessary job prerequisite, such work acquaints one with an institution and provides an advantage over someone who does not have this background.

Homemakers—men and women who perform various duties required to take care of a home, which may include caring for the children of a working couple—can learn their duties on the job. If homemaking appeals to you, but you do not know what is expected, offer to work for someone who will train you in the home for a limited time. Actually, many nurses seek such part-time jobs when hospitals have to cut back on nursing schedules.

Unlicensed health aides are somewhat like homemakers. Patients who are sick, incapacitated, or recuperating from an accident or operation may require the services of someone who can be with them to help them dress, go to the bathroom, bathe, and even eat. Such a patient does not require skilled nursing care, or if needed on a limited basis, a home health agency or visiting nurse association can provide the necessary professional assistance.

When Carrie Goldsfarb left high school, she was not sure that she wanted to train for a position in health care. She decided to work in the field but not invest time and money for training until she was certain about such a career. She found a position acting as a companion to an elderly woman disabled by arthritis, but otherwise in good health. Carrie found it challenging and rewarding to help the woman prepare meals, do light cleaning, and shop. Based on this experience, she decided that caring for others would offer personally satisfying career possibilities and enrolled in a nursing course.

Training Available While You Work

Most cities and many towns offer a wide scope of job training courses for those who want to acquire new skills while working.

Night school was the traditional training ground for immigrants who arrived in eastern seaboard cities. Unfamiliar with the language, they were eligible only for the lowest-paid jobs. History tells us how these courageous, hard-working, and determined men and women struggled to get an education, and many of them eventually rose to top-level positions in business, industry, and their chosen professions. They could do it then; anyone can do it today. Night school at community colleges and vocational or training schools still enables Americans to learn new skills each year.

On-the-job training is available in some institutions. Some farsighted employers agree to arrange working schedules to enable employees to take daytime courses that are otherwise not available. Some employers will even pay tuition fees for employees eager to improve themselves. The administrator of a large private hospital in the Southeast encouraged CNAs on staff to take daytime courses that would eventually allow them to become certified as LPNs.

Correspondence or home study courses leading to a certificate or even a college degree are always a possibility. The Distance Education and Training Council provides a wide range of information. You'll find the mailing address and website listed at the end of this chapter.

A good time to improve yourself is between jobs. Since Enrico Caprizi was ten years old, he wanted to become an emergency medical technician because he had seen a team in action. His family, however, would hear nothing of it and pointed him toward a banking career. Working as a teller, he managed to save enough to enable him to resign and pay for his EMT training and living expenses until he could finish school and obtain permanent employment.

Financial Help May Be Available

There's no such thing as a free lunch. However, those who need financial help to attend school may be surprised to find that it is sometimes possible to obtain a scholarship or student loan to help finance their training or education. Alec Studley wanted to become a therapist but lacked the necessary funds to continue his education after high school. He learned that a state program would pay his tuition as well as provide a small stipend toward his living expenses while in school. This made it possible to realize his ambition.

If you need financial assistance, first check the school catalog for such information and discuss your needs with the director of admissions or the administrator. If your search for aid is unsuccessful, inquire at the public library and your state's Department of Education. They may have helpful information or can direct you to the proper agency. Those bound for college, either undergraduate or graduate, should consult the books listed in the next section.

For Further Information

Organizations

Accrediting Commission of Career Schools and Colleges of
Technology
2101 Wilson Boulevard, Suite 302
Arlington, VA 22201
www.accsct.org

The Distance Education and Training Council
1601 Eighteenth Street NW
Washington, DC 20009
www.detc.org

Suggested Reading

Cassidy, Daniel J. *The Scholarship Book: The Complete Guide to
Private-Sector Scholarships, Grants, and Loans for
Undergraduates* (5th edition). Englewood Cliffs, NJ: Prentice-
Hall, 1996.

Eberts, Marjorie, and Margaret Gisler. *Careers for Good
Samaritans and Other Humanitarian Types.* Chicago: VGM
Career Books, 1998.

Kerby, Debra M. *Fund Your Way Through College: Uncovering
1,700 Great Opportunities in Undergraduate Financial Aid.*
Detroit: Visible Ink Press, 1994.

Peterson's Paying Less for College (13th edition). Princeton, NJ:
Peterson's Guides, 1996.

CHAPTER THREE

Caregiving in Hospitals

Attempts at health care reform seem to be a regular fixture of each legislative session in the United States. Unlike Canada, where there is national health coverage for all, many U.S. citizens do not have access to affordable health care. While most changes in U.S. policy never make it to the president's desk, changes in the industry are always taking place.

Consider the following statistics: A few years ago, normal pregnancies required a two-to-three-day hospitalization. Today, some health maintenance organizations (HMOs) consider twenty-four hours sufficient. In 1980, 15 percent of all surgeries were carried out on an outpatient basis; by 1986, 25 percent of all surgery nationwide was performed on an outpatient basis. In 1993, the figure was 50 percent. And now in the early part of the new century, we see the statistic hovering at 75 percent. Quite a trend.

Currently, many hospitals are reporting that their average number of inpatient days continues a steady downward trend. There are a number of reasons for this decline, including improvements in surgical techniques, better infection control, and the fact that many people are postponing elective surgery because they lack health insurance, do not want to take sick leave for a nonessential operation, or the fact that insurers insist on short stays.

Major improvements in the health care industry have occurred and will continue to occur, and nowhere will this be more evident than in the nation's hospitals. The economy and the insurance industry have forced most institutions, even the most successful ones, to seek new ways to survive.

Many hospital administrators are looking for solutions in merging institutions serving the same or contiguous communities, eliminating competing services, and making more efficient use of physicians and other medical specialists.

Hospitals Are Reaching Out

More and more, hospitals are incorporating nontraditional methods and services into their usual caregiving responsibilities. They are promoting preventive care and wellness services and are taking advantage of dynamic partnerships with other institutions, sometimes even in other countries, to provide better care for all patients.

Networking

New York Hospital, which is affiliated with the Cornell Medical Center, is one of the most distinguished teaching hospitals in the nation. When Dr. David B. Skinner became president and chief executive officer in 1987, the crumbling hospital, built a half-century before, was losing more than $1 million a week. Within three years, Dr. Skinner turned the $47.2 million annual loss to a surplus of $2 million.

Today, the hospital is part of the New York Hospital Care Network, a complex arrangement with other institutions such as hospitals, clinics, and nursing homes in the city and adjoining Westchester County. Forming such an extensive network has achieved substantial cost savings as well as generally improved health care. "I think our network structure provides us with the flexibility to offer top quality care no matter what," Dr. Skinner told a *New York Times* reporter.

Wellness and Diversified Services

Did you think that hospitals are only for the sick, the injured, and the dying? If so, you're quite wrong! Today, many hospitals have broadened their missions to stress *wellness*, a term that may include yoga, meditation, aerobics, physical fitness and workout centers, health clubs with steam rooms, and jogging programs. One hospital offers belly dancing classes; another, writing courses for stress management. At one prominent hospital, an average of five times more patients use the fitness center than lie in acute care. To show you how far one institution has gone to cultivate good community relations, it even offers free testing for blood pressure, cholesterol, and other medical problems.

"Why all these activities?" you may ask. The answer is that the specter of health reform is always looming—changes in the law could create a system where hospitals would be paid a lump sum to provide care to a group of people. Thus, it is to the hospital's advantage to keep people well and loyal to the institution so that if they do get sick, they will choose the hospital that provided a wellness program.

Wellness is not a new concept. Some hospitals started programs in the 1970s, but the hospital-sponsored fitness and health club programs did not spread until late in the 1980s. One hospital in Virginia has some four hundred residents coming daily for physical and social activities. It has become almost a community center, even holding an after-prom party for high school graduates that lasted until dawn. In another hospital, karate, tai chi, and meditation courses, as well as weight loss and smoking-cessation courses, are offered.

Has this paid off? Indeed it has! A spokesperson for the Association of Health and Fitness Centers said that at some large hospitals, wellness programs earn as much as half a million dollars in profit annually!

An Overall View

According to the American Hospital Association, the nation's approximately fifty-eight hundred hospitals fall into three broad classifications:

1. Nonprofit, operated by communities, churches, or fraternal institutions
2. Governmental, consisting of federal hospitals, state, county, and municipal institutions
3. Proprietary or private hospitals operated for profit

There is one further distinction among hospitals you will want to know if you are interested in a hospital career. Most hospitals are devoted just to patient care and are not equipped to teach medical or nursing personnel. These are usually private institutions or are located in isolated areas where affiliation with universities or schools of nursing would not be practical. They are service hospitals.

"Teaching" hospitals are devoted to not only serving patients but also permitting medical students to work and study under teacher-physician supervisors, because so much patient care is learned through actual practice. These institutions have developed training programs within their organizations structured toward that end.

Employment Opportunities

Employees of hospitals run the gamut from the most highly trained neurosurgeons to volunteer high school students. The wide range of jobs available means that there is the need for an equally wide range of people, from those with advanced degrees to those with a high school education. Quite a few of the jobs in hospitals do not require professional training. Many skills can be learned on the job—nurse's aide, messenger, stock clerk, waiter, dishwasher, housekeeper, porter, laundry sorter, floor polisher. Some of the positions call for skills you can learn while in high school, trade school, through special courses taken after high school, or through apprenticeship. These jobs include switchboard operator, bookkeeper, painter, baker, electrician, and tailors. Professional positions such as administrator, pharmacist, librarian, computer specialist, or dietitian call for more extensive training, or even graduate work.

Possible Job Titles

Listed below are the more common classifications for hospital employees in administration and plant operation positions.

ADMINISTRATIVE
Administrator
Assistant administrator
Public relations director
Volunteer services director
Computer services director
Patients' librarian
Stenographer
Medical transcriptionist
Receptionist
Messenger
Medical photographer
Medical secretary
General secretary
Clerks (mail, file, payroll, inventory, accounts payable and
    receivable, and office clerks in special departments)
Switchboard operator

ADMITTING
Admitting officer
Admitting clerk

BUSINESS OFFICE
Controller-business manager
Accountant
Credit manager
Bookkeeper
Cashier

PERSONNEL
Personnel director
Employment interviewer
Job analyst

PURCHASING
Purchasing officer
Stockroom manager
Stock clerk

PROFESSIONAL SERVICE
Anesthesia and inhalation therapy
Nurse anesthetist
Inhalation therapy technician

CLINICAL LABORATORIES AND RELATED FACILITIES
Biochemist
Bacteriologist
Blood bank supervisor
Serologist
Laboratory technician
Laboratory assistant
Medical technologist

DIETARY
Director of dietetics
Therapeutic dietitian
Baker

Counter server
Dishwasher
Chef
Cook
Cafeteria manager
Waiter

MEDICAL LIBRARY
Medical librarian

MEDICAL RECORDS
Medical record librarian
Medical record clerk

NURSING EDUCATION
Director
Assistant director
Instructor

NURSING SERVICE
Director
Assistant director
Supervisor
Head nurse
General duty nurse
Practical nurse
Nurse's aide
Orderly
Nursing unit clerk

PHARMACY
Chief pharmacist
Registered pharmacist
Pharmacy technician

RADIOLOGY
Registered x-ray technician
Ultrasound technician

REHABILITATION
Physical therapist
Director of occupational or physical therapy department
Occupational therapist
Occupational or physical therapy aide

SOCIAL SERVICE
Director of social service
Psychiatric social worker
Medical social worker
Casework aide

ENGINEERING AND MAINTENANCE
Chief hospital engineer
Assistant engineer
Firefighter
Electrician
Carpenter
Elevator repair person
Mason-plasterer
Painter
Plumber

HOUSEKEEPING
Executive housekeeper
Housekeeping supervisor
Seamstress
Linen room control clerk
Maid
Porter

Floor polisher
Wall and window washer

LAUNDRY
Laundry manager
Marker
Ironer
Presser
Sorter
Washer

The following provides further description of some of the common career paths within the hospital setting. These wide-ranging careers require varying levels of education and training and cover all major departments found in hospitals.

Administrator

The job of hospital administrator is one of the most complex in the entire health field. He or she is responsible for the care and maintenance of all operations and facilities of the hospital. This may involve direct supervision of as many as thirty-two main departments.

The administrator has three main divisions of responsibility: administrative, professional and technical, and nontechnical. In the administrative role, the administrator must act as the supervisor of activities, such as admissions, communications, information, personnel, and purchasing.

In the professional and technical role, the administrator must consider activities that contribute directly to the patients' welfare by delegating authority to the various department heads and trained technicians.

In the nontechnical role, the administrator supervises the maintenance and care of the building and its facilities, as well as the operation of the hospital.

Some of the administrator's principal day-to-day responsibilities include:

- Maintaining an accurate and efficient accounting system, including preparing periodic budgets and detailed financial statements
- Recruiting all hospital personnel, including nurses, pharmacists, janitors, laundry workers, technicians, and so forth, and providing for all the physicians and surgeons who work within the hospital
- Selecting, purchasing, and financing all of the hospital supplies, making certain that the hospital has the best and most up-to-date equipment it can afford
- Coordinating the work of all the departments and seeing that hospital policies are carried out by the entire staff
- Supervising the planning and operation of teaching programs for student nurses and other in-service programs for other staff members
- Acting as the link between the entire hospital staff and the Board of Trustees or other governing body

Although four years of college plus graduate work is now the most typical method of entering the field, it is possible to gain experience in various hospital positions and work your way up to the top jobs. Those employed in similar administrative work in hotels, sanitariums, schools, prisons, public administration, and business may find it possible to transfer.

Admitting Officer

This member of the administrative staff receives and interviews new patients, makes room reservations, and keeps a complete index of all patients and records of all available beds.

For this position, a four-year college degree is preferred, although it is not a requirement.

Hospital Dietitian

The hospital dietitian's job is important and complex because of the tremendous advances in the sciences of nutrition and food service administration over the past several decades. In place of a single dietitian, who once served an entire hospital, a large institution may have a number of dietitians, each of whom is a specialist in a different field.

Approximately half of all trained dietitians serve in hospitals, but you will also find many opportunities for dietitians outside hospitals. Dietitians manage school food-service programs, direct college and university food services, and hold positions with industrial firms, hotels, restaurants, tearooms, and transportation companies. Some dietitians have encouraged broader understanding of good nutrition through books and television appearances.

You must earn a bachelor's degree from an accredited college or university, and it is recommended that you have one year of postgraduate work in a dietetic internship approved by the American Dietetic Association. Although you will find employment opportunities after receiving your B.S. or B.A., this further study is a logical part of your preparation. Completion of your internship qualifies you for membership in this professional association.

The hospital dietetics field can be divided into five main categories: food-service administration or management, diet therapy, clinical diatetics, teaching, and research.

Food Service Administration and Management. If you have a special interest in and aptitude for management, you might enjoy supervising the preparation and service of all meals for patients and hospital personnel. In addition, you would be responsible for personnel relations in your department, teaching employees, purchasing food and equipment, maintaining standards of sanitation, and supervising the food and labor cost accounting. As an administrative dietitian, you would work very closely with the administrator of your hospital.

Diet Therapy. This career path can prove intriguing because it calls for planning both normal and modified diets to meet the individual needs of your patients as prescribed by their physicians. You would help patients understand why it is necessary for them to follow therapeutic diets and show them how to fit diets into their everyday lives at home.

Clinical Dietetics. This branch of the profession appeals to dietitians who like to give nutritional guidance to patients. These patients are not hospitalized but are referred by doctors, who want them to understand the diets that have been prescribed for them. A clinical dietitian may also teach classes for expectant mothers, diabetics, overweight people, and others who have nutritional problems.

Teaching. Giving instruction is a part of almost all dietetic work, but you will find that full-time positions are available to dietitians in hospitals that have schools of nursing and provide instruction for medical and dental students and dietetic interns.

In a small hospital you would, of course, find entirely different working conditions. Here, you might be the only member of the staff trained in dietetics, with no professional to whom you could delegate many of your responsibilities. However, such a job could be both challenging and fun. Some dietitians serve two or more small hospitals in the same community. They are referred to as shared dietitians.

Research. Clinical research activities are usually conducted in large hospitals affiliated with medical centers.

A research dietitian works closely with patients, doctors, nurses, and chemists. It is her task to calculate diets according to orders of the physicians, but also to make certain that they are acceptable to the patients. A common type of research is the balance study, a time-consuming procedure. It entails computing a constant diet in which quantitative analysis is applied to the patient's intake as well as output. This calls for careful supervision of food preparation and consumption.

Executive Housekeeper

Usually the person in this position is responsible for the cleanliness of the hospital and for the provision and maintenance of bed linens and clothing. He or she must see that walls and windows are spotless, floors polished, furniture dusted, and bathrooms, laboratories, and all equipment maintained. In addition, this person will see that rooms are repainted and repairs made as needed, and that housekeeping and janitorial service are available. Executive housekeepers often supervise the laundry, which may have a separate staff and manager.

Hospital Engineer

This individual usually acts as engineer and superintendent of plant operation. He or she makes certain that all operating equipment is in good condition, the building well heated, lighted, and in good repair, and that the grounds are well maintained. For this career path, some college work will be required, and for large institutions, an advanced degree in engineering would be required.

Medical Librarian

Medical librarians organize and administer collections of books and journals. An enormous amount of literature is published in the medical field, probably more than in any other. It is estimated that approximately nine thousand medical journals are published annually. Duties of the medical librarian include:

- Selecting, acquiring, and cataloging books and journals
- Assisting and furthering the education, reading, and research of those using the library

- Rendering reference, bibliographic, and interlibrary loan services
- Instructing the library clientele in the use of the catalog, special reference tools, and indexes

In order to become a medical librarian, you need four years of college, plus a master of library science degree from a school of library science. Some approved library schools offer courses in medical librarianship. Scholarships are also available. The Medical Library Association includes membership for individuals and institutions.

Medical Record Librarian or Health Information Technician

This is a new and growing field and, because of the shortage of medical-record librarians, is a profession you may want to consider. In fact, the 2000–2001 *Occupation Outlook Handbook* projects "Health Information Technician" to be one of the twenty fastest-growing occupations. In this job, you work alongside members of clinical staffs and medical specialists, reviewing, as well as coordinating and organizing, their extensive reports, making them ready for immediate use. Specifically, the following are some of the tasks of a registered medical record librarian:

- Review patients' records for completeness and accuracy in accordance with certain accepted standards
- Code diseases, operations, and special treatments according to a recognized classification system
- Index diseases, operations, and other special study material
- Assist the medical staff in research involving medical records for specific purposes of the hospital or clinic
- Answer inquiries for information recorded in patients' records

- Participate in staff meetings representing a professional service and represent the hospital or clinic and other medical-legal activities
- Prepare periodic narrative and statistical presentations on the overall utilization of the hospital or clinic

Employment opportunities include positions such as directors, assistant directors, and assistant or staff medical record librarians. All of these openings are found in hospitals, clinics, research institutions, and government-operated institutions. Instructors or lecturers are needed in hospitals with in-service educational programs, as are medical record consultants.

To become a medical record librarian, you need four years of college, leading to a bachelor's degree in medical record library science or a similar degree, or a minimum of two years of undergraduate work plus a one-year approved hospital course in medical record library science. At the conclusion of either preparatory program, students may take the examination for registration conducted by the American Health Information Management Association.

Those unable to afford three or four years of study following high school, may take a nine-month course in basic medical-record technology, as offered in certain approved hospital schools, and combine classroom instruction with on-the-job training. This special preparation leads to proficiency in the technical and clerical aspects of medical record work. There are many excellent positions within medical record departments for trained medical record technicians who work under the direction of professional medical record librarians.

Aide (CNA or Orderly)

Aides feed patients, assist in bathing them, straighten the rooms, and do any other tasks that contribute to a patient's comfort.

Employers prefer that applicants have a high school diploma; training is provided on the job or in a vocational-technical school.

Receptionist

The receptionist is usually the person who answers questions and gives directions to visitors, controls passes, takes messages, and receives packages and flowers for patients. He or she may also assist at the switchboard and perform minor clerical duties. Again, a high school diploma is preferred, as are typing and computer skills.

....

The Future for Hospitals

Some economists and health specialists argue we have too many hospital beds and must weed out the surplus, inefficient, and unnecessary institutions. Between 1972 and 1990, the number of hospital beds shrank 22 percent. At the same time, many mental patients were evicted from hospitals and ended up homeless. Health care costs had risen so quickly that people could not afford to go to hospitals, and states had no money to pay for institutionalized patients. It was at this time that our country began the great debate over universal health care coverage. The effort to begin a nationalized health program where all citizens would have access to and insurance for health-related expenses created much controversy for the Clinton administration and ultimately failed.

If universal health care insurance were to appear on the horizon again, hospitals would probably not have a glut of beds, but would suddenly find themselves overwhelmed by the pent-up demand. Whether such a thing will occur is up to the president and Congress. But since lack of insurance and skyrocketing medical expenses are a perpetual complaint, it seems likely to be an issue in the hospital industry's future. For those interested in careers in hospitals, the future looks good; but bear in mind the warning stated by Philip Ryan, president of Health Northeast, a hospital holding company: "In the future we will be slower to add full-time people. We will be using more contract employees and per diem arrangements, so it won't be so difficult to adjust to changes in patient volume."

Clearly, as in many industries today, the trend has already become the norm, but down the road, the overall employment outlook would seem to justify consideration of a career in our nation's hospital industry. Because the hospital arena is such a large employer, even slower-than-average growth still means a huge number of new jobs.

. . . .

For Further Information

Organizations

American Health Information Management Association
233 North Michigan Avenue, Suite 2150
Chicago, IL 60601
www.ahima.org

American Hospital Association
One Franklin, 28th Floor
Chicago, IL 60606
www.hospitalconnect.com

Health Canada
Address Locator 1908A1
Ottawa, ON K1A 1B4
Canada
www.hc-sc.gc.ca

CHAPTER FOUR

Caregiving in Nursing Homes

One of every eight senior citizens will enter a nursing home where that resident will probably live out the rest of his or her life. In the health care industry, the preferred terms are *patient* in a hospital and *resident* in a nursing home or other non-hospital setting.

For the most part nursing homes cater to the elderly. However, because hospitals have begun to mandate shorter and shorter patient stays, many younger men and women must also transfer from a hospital to a nursing home to convalesce from an illness or operation.

When you consider that the "graying of America" is increasing the ranks of those baby boomers over sixty-five from 32 million in 1990 to a projected high of 70 million in the year 2030, and that by the same year, our nursing home population is expected to double, you will have some idea of the size and importance of the nursing home industry. In 2002, there were more than 17,000 nursing homes caring for some 1.5 million older adults. The 1999 National Nursing Home Survey (Center for Disease Control, National Center for Health Statistics) showed 66.5 percent of nursing homes were proprietary (for profit), 26.7 percent were voluntary nonprofit, and 6.7 percent were run by government agencies or "other."

Now, step back and look at this from another perspective. Nursing home operation is an important industry. Today there are well over 1.5 million residents who pay a minimum of $100 to $225 a day, or from $36,500 a year to $82,000 per year. Many of these residents receive help from their insurance companies or from Medicaid. Nursing home operators are making bank deposits in the billions annually. Little wonder many enterprising entrepreneurs have moved in to share the profits!

It is no secret that many seniors declare they would rather die than enter a nursing home. That feeling partly results from the poor reputation many nursing homes have earned, as well as a person's realization that, in most cases, when taken to a home, "This is where I go to die."

It is true that there are certainly examples of privately owned nursing homes where the bottom line is profit rather than care and where residents can suffer because of inadequate staffing. However, this is not true of all homes, for there are many fine institutions throughout the country. Nevertheless, the emphasis on profit can be a problem for the resident as much as for the caregiver.

Elise Robinson, a young and enthusiastic practical nurse, applied for a position in a new nursing home. It was a beautiful facility, well equipped, nicely furnished, and sparkling clean throughout. Yet, she found her working conditions intolerable. Not only was she greatly overworked during the 11 P.M. to 7 A.M. shift to which she was initially assigned, but she could not tolerate being part of a team that was unable to give residents the care they needed. She and the one aide assisting her could not keep up with all the calls for help.

Because this might happen to you, if you are seeking a position in a nursing home—regardless of whether it is a public institution, privately owned, profit or nonprofit—check around the community to learn all you can about the home's reputation. If possible, talk with members of the staff, people who have had family or friends staying there, or ex-residents.

Although possible staffing problems exist, a majority of these institutions are well managed and adequately staffed, conscientiously caring for their residents. One such institution is the Grafton County Nursing Home.

··

Grafton County Nursing Home

"You'll never believe what I did for my master's project." Judith Lupien's eyes sparkled as she chuckled in her office in the Grafton County Nursing Home. Judith is one of two social workers responsible for the home's social services and public relations functions as well as admissions and resident advocacy, a broad management assignment.

The Grafton County Nursing Home perches high on a ridge overlooking the Connecticut Valley. The original building, constructed in 1930, is an attractive three-story colonial brick structure with an overhanging roof supported by imposing, tall white pillars. Combined with a more modern wing, added in 1969, the home offers intermediate nursing care to approximately 135 residents (including a twenty-bed Alzheimer's, or "Special Needs," Unit).

"I really stuck my neck out," Judith continued as she explained that she chose to ask more than a dozen residents, a good cross section, this question: "If you could be granted one wish, what would it be?"

"This was not idle curiosity," she said. "Rather, it was a long-felt desire to learn more about the men and women who, for one reason or another, must spend the last years of their lives in an institutional setting. Our health care system assumes it knows what is best for them. But do we really know what is missing or how we might make their lives happier by including them in decisions that affect their lives and give them control over their lives in general?

"My professor agreed that the thesis might make a significant contribution to this aspect of the health care field, and it did!

Since 1985, after the completion of this special project for my gerontology course and my master's degree, this project resulted in a 'mushroom effect,' where so many more people have gotten involved and have added quality of life for these special people. Today, it still goes on."

The results were indeed surprising. The wishes ranged from the elderly man who just wanted a new toothbrush and his favorite toothpaste to the woman who wanted to go to Maine to see the ocean to the disabled woman who said, "I long to return to my old home." A few other wishes were: "An evening gown and a place to wear it"; "To have my room fixed up, new curtains"; "To go fishing in a boat"; "To eat in a restaurant."

When asked if it were possible to make many wishes come true, Judith exclaimed, "Absolutely! Every one! My husband and I took the woman over to Maine for a weekend; we managed to persuade the family of the disabled woman to accept her return for a weekend; and we were able to make every other wish come true." She explained that generous benefactors in the community helped make wishes possible, and those same donors provided funds for many other activities planned for the residents, which could not be met by the nursing home's operating budget.

This was not a new undertaking for Judith. During the more than sixteen years she spent at a state-run nursing home, she was instrumental in organizing trips to the theater, concerts, recreational areas, shopping, and other places geared to the interests of the residents. In addition, she did what she could to help brighten the lives of those who were physically unable to leave the home by using volunteers representing forty-eight groups and organizations from all over the state.

Helping to improve residents' quality of life and acting as the home's public relations representative are not all that Judith does. As admissions coordinator, she spends much of her time interviewing and counseling family members and others who seek to place a relative or friend in the home. Interviews are usually combined with a complete tour of the facility—something she generously gave us. It is obvious that she enjoys her work and is proud of the institution and all the caregivers who work there.

She said that the workforce of about thirty includes an administrator, office staff, registered and practical nurses, CNAs, housekeepers, laundry workers, a dietitian, cooks, custodians, and maintenance and activity personnel. Since July 1990, the administrator, John P. Richwagen, has brought a background of hospital administrative experience to the nursing home operation. John said that perhaps his philosophy on the proper environment for a nursing home was best expressed in the brochure given to prospective residents and their family members. It is reproduced here because, for those interested in this aspect of caregiving, it is one of the best descriptions of what a nursing home should and could be.

OUR SUPPORTIVE ENVIRONMENT

Our nursing home has changed greatly in recent years to meet the changing needs of residents. We always have worked hard to meet residents' physical needs and activities of daily living. We have built an excellent reputation for our caring atmosphere. Now, in addition, we are emphasizing residents' choices as to activities, foods, and other services.

This approach enhances residents' quality of life, dignity, and control over their lives. We encourage residents to dress, walk, if possible, participate in individual and group activities, and have visitors. This encourages independence and functioning to the highest possible level—our primary mission. Many extras at our home are available, thanks to donations received from the Grafton County Home Association.

OUR CARING STAFF

Our staff provides a multidisciplinary approach to resident care. Members of nursing, social services, dietary, staff development, activities, and administration meet regularly with residents and their family members to discuss their care, concerns, and goals. It is our belief that each resident is a unique person in his or her own right with likes and dislikes, abilities, and needs. We focus on each resident's unique individuality and abilities.

Our caring staff receives frequently conducted training designed to meet specific needs of residents. Such training is conducted for all departments and all staff members. This emphasis on training and education, we find, boosts employee morale, skills, and knowledge, and enhances the quality of care for residents as the end result. We are very proud of our excellent, dedicated, caring staff.

SPECIAL NEEDS UNIT

We recognize that people suffering from Alzheimer's disease and related disorders have very special needs. We, therefore, designed our Special Needs Unit to provide a safe, secure, and comfortable environment for these residents. Our staff has received special training in activities and interventions to enable residents in this unit to function to the extent possible, maintain some control over their lives, and retain dignity and quality of life.

Located in a private wing, our SNU offers custom renovations and selective furnishings to meet residents' needs. A sunny, spacious atrium looks out on our garden. This is a pleasant setting for dining, activities, or just relaxing. We offer support for family members and caregivers who become an extended part of the resident's family.

OUR HOME IS YOUR HOME

In many parts of the world, a vital part of hospitality is to make people feel at home. This is our philosophy, too. Every aspect of our care for residents is to provide as home-like an atmosphere as possible. This includes our special living environment, our well-trained staff, and supportive services. Our philosophy is to enable residents to function at the highest level possible and maintain control over their lives. We combine medical knowledge and excellent care with commonsense "people" skills to achieve this objective. We also encourage family members to be part of our care team.

To encourage residents to be as independent as possible, special services offered include: trips by wheelchair van to go shopping, for ice cream, to watch ball games, view Christmas lights and fall foliage. Special events are held each month with a special theme, and picnics outside are provided in summer.

Many county nursing homes have their roots in the old-time poorhouses and county homes. Thus, some of these institutions may have a poor image among that segment of the public that has had no contact with these facilities. The perception that government cannot deliver services comparable to or even better than the private sector is not necessarily true, as demonstrated by the staff and administrators of Grafton County Nursing Home.

Some nursing homes set aside special rooms with private baths for patients who do not need nursing care but no longer can prepare their meals or do normal housekeeping chores. This is called "assisted living" or "supportive living." There are numerous "supportive living" homes that are not connected with nursing homes but provide the same essential services for those who are able to take care of themselves and walk without assistance.

Caregivers for Supportive Living

The sign, "Bittersweet Inn—A Shared Home for Loved Elderly," stood along the driveway of the large, white, three-story colonial house. A single-story ell connected the main building with a huge barn, making this a typically charming New England farm complex. At one side, the corn towered over a large vegetable garden and a flower garden surrounded by bird feeders.

A stately woman with gray hair walked over to greet us.

"I'm Mrs. Taylor, one of the residents," she announced. "Looking for Brenda Bachmann?"

"Yes, please."

She nodded toward the house. "You'll find her in the living room. Can't miss her because she's petite, pretty, blonde, and," she paused and smiled almost mischievously, "she's cute as a bug's ear!"

A moment later, the woman so accurately described greeted us at the door. "I'm so pleased you could come. Let me show you around our home. By the way, call me Brenda. We like informality here."

As we made the usual small talk following introductions, we noted that the attractive large living room had wide floorboards that ran the width of the room and contrasted nicely with the rich burgundy curtains. A mauve rose-floral overstuffed sofa and several cherry wingback chairs with end tables standing on a rose-ivory rug made an inviting setting.

She led us into the formal dining room, which was furnished with a cherry table and matching chairs. The mint-green walls complemented the dark green floor with its trailing ivy motif. A four-tiered chandelier complemented the white, floor-length, hand-crocheted tablecloth; the table was set for eight with a service of "Old Rose" patterned china.

"We've tried to restore and furnish the house as it might have been back in 1840 and decided to use cherry furniture," she explained. "You will notice we have antiques throughout the house, and every bed has a Raggedy Ann and Raggedy Andy because I'm a collector."

Opening a door to a wide hallway, she took us down to a cheerful bedroom furnished with a high four-poster bed and matching cherry bureaus. On one wall there was a small fireplace, an easy chair with a bridge lamp, and a small table; a bookcase completed the homey furnishings.

"This is our only room with a private bath," Brenda said. "The other three residents, who are on the second floor and have single rooms, share the bathroom." We followed her upstairs to see the lounge area with its television and the bedrooms, each of which was decorated and furnished in a different style. Then we visited the spotless kitchen and proceeded on to the ell connected to the barn.

"Someday we plan to convert this part of the house into three or four guest rooms, each with bath," Brenda told us. When we walked into the barn, she laughed as she waved her arm. "And think what we will do with this!" The barn, with its hand-hewn haylofts and wooden flooring, had a nostalgic scent of hay and cows. "Actually," she continued, "I would love to have a nursing home wing, and this would be ideal for that purpose."

We asked why she had not set aside some rooms for that now. She explained that state regulations require a sprinkler system. Furthermore, it would be necessary to purchase other equipment, which she did not need for a supportive living home.

While relaxing outdoors on the deck, Brenda talked about her background. "For many years, I had a close and loving relationship with my grandparents, which gave me both experience and insight into the needs of the elderly. I still share that closeness with my maternal grandmother, and I wanted to share it with others, too. All I know is older people. I like caring for them more than younger men and women, although I brought up two children of my own.

"My greatest wish has always been to have a home where I could provide top-notch care for older people who would spend the last years of their lives with me. To prepare for this, I became a CNA; I worked in institutions and also as a private duty nurse and saved my money. Fortunately, Rod, my husband, who is a doctor, shared my dream and has helped me all along the way. We needed his income when we were planning this home because of the start-up expenses, to say nothing of the huge investment needed for furniture and equipment."

Brenda has someone to help with the housework as well as an aide to look after the residents' needs. "Our inn is a 'home away from home,' where residents are a family unit, living in a caring atmosphere that fosters dignity and independence," the owner said. "We provide services and support in the least restrictive normal living environment possible, because ours is a noninstitutional private home setting where residents come by choice to live."

The cook prepares all meals, and on his days off, the aide and Brenda cook and serve. When the aide is not there, Brenda covers for her. Sometimes some of the residents offer to help, which gives them a sense of being needed.

In addition to running the inn, Brenda finds time to plan activities for the residents, take them to the doctor, the mall, the movies, or a drive into the mountains. As if that is not enough, she is also a licensed cosmetologist and can take care of the residents' beauty needs.

As we prepared to leave, we asked Brenda if she had any advice for those interested in starting their own assisted care home.

"Yes, indeed," she said without hesitating. "First, make sure you like to work with the elderly. Remember it's not like working an eight-hour shift in a hospital or nursing home. It's twenty-four hours, seven days a week, four weeks a month. If you are certain you can do this, then get some kind of nursing training and experience. Find out what your state requires to run a home—whether you must be a CNA, a practical, or a registered nurse. Obtain your training, then get experience working in nursing or assisted living homes, and later, if you have the money, open your own!"

Life-Care Community

One of the latest developments for geriatric care is the life-care community or continuing-care retirement community. Although not a nursing home per se, life-care communities do offer guaranteed nursing care for those who are able to afford it. The advantage of the life-care concept is that nursing care is given within the resident's home, which is part of a large housing complex. If more extensive nursing is needed, the infirmary is also part of the complex and is always accessible—convenient for a visiting spouse.

The typical facility sells apartment condominiums to qualifying couples or single persons and guarantees to provide them care for life (except when residents are compelled to seek skilled hospital services). Most centers offer meals, housekeeping, maintenance, health and recreational facilities, and an infirmary where residents may go for medical treatment and unlimited nursing care.

Life-care facilities are springing up wherever there are enough people who desire this unique lifestyle and have the means to support it. Employment possibilities are numerous, ranging from cooks, kitchen assistants, and waitpersons for the dining room and coffee shop to custodians, housekeepers, administrators and support staff, as well as nurses, geriatric aides, nursing aides, and maintenance crews.

To find life-care facilities in your area, look in the Yellow Pages under "Retirement and Life-Care Communities and Homes."

The Nursing Home Revolution

Traditional nursing homes are reinventing themselves because it has become obvious to many administrators that they will have to remain competitive with the home health and other agencies that provide direct care to the sick in their residences. Furthermore, the ever-widening array of alternative care facilities for the elderly is emptying nursing home beds. A third factor is that since so many seniors want to avoid going to a nursing home, the smart nursing home administrators have asked the question: "Why not bring us to the patient?"

Here are three examples of what has happened:

1. A nursing home in Brooklyn, New York, offers visiting nurses and day care to people still living in their homes. A respite program permits caregivers who need to get away for a day or longer to leave the patient in the nursing home's care. A long-term health plan provided for one patient sent a home health aide to her daily, five days a week; a nurse checked the patient every two weeks; a senior nurse reevaluated her health care plan every four months; a laboratory technician performed blood tests monthly; and a social worker visited when needed.

2. In Danbury, Connecticut, a nursing home opened an apartment complex for older people on the nursing home grounds. Services offered to these residents included housekeeping; a delivered daily meal; transportation to doctors/dentists and shopping; an emergency call system; and other assistance. Residents receive medical care in the nursing home and, when no longer able to care for themselves, can transfer to the nursing facility.

3. A third nursing home in Woodland, California, has a "personal security business," which enables older people in the community to have the home check on them daily.

Subacute care is another nontraditional service many nursing homes are adding. Subacute care provides treatment for chronic diseases, broken bones, and similar problems that do not require hospital diagnosis or surgery. In doing this, nursing homes are able to save patients and insurance companies higher hospital charges, as well as serve young people, thus eliminating the need to depend on geriatric patients to fill their beds.

This is another manifestation of the tremendous change taking place in health care, which will offer additional career opportunities for a wide range of caregivers.

For Further Information

Organizations

American Health Care Association
1201 L Street NW
Washington, DC 20005
www.ahca.org

American Hospital Association
Division of Nursing
One North Franklin
Chicago, IL 60606
www.aha.org

Health Canada
Division of Aging Seniors
Population Health Directorate
Address Locator 1908A1
Ottawa, ON K1A 1B4
Canada
www.hc-sc.gc.ca/seniors-aines
www.eldercarehomehealth.com *(Toronto only)*

The Care Guide
9 Cedarview Drive
West Hill, ON M1C 2K5
Canada
www.thecareguide.com
   (Canada's senior housing and care services.)

Suggested Reading

Williams, Ellen. *Opportunities in Gerontology and Aging Services Careers.* Chicago: VGM Career Books, 2002.

CHAPTER FIVE

Caregiving in Senior Day-Care Centers

D ay-care centers are recognized as an important part of the health field. Medicaid covers expenses for those unable to pay in almost all states, and long-term care insurance policies now include day care. There is growing evidence that adult day-care centers lower the depression often experienced by the elderly.

In a medium-size town in northern Florida, the senior citizen minivan made its first stop at the home of an elderly couple who were waiting at the curb. At his wife's urging, the man finally climbed into the car and settled uneasily into the back seat. He appeared normal but he had Alzheimer's disease, and this trip to the day-care center for seniors gave him a change. More important, it provided a respite for his wife from constantly coping with his frequent dementia and failing memory.

At the next stop, an elderly woman in a wheelchair expertly guided herself onto the lift, which raised her up into the van. For this widow, the outing provided much-needed companionship and a hot noon meal. At the last two stops, the van picked up a man and a woman, both of whom were living with their adult daughters.

The center, formerly a small private home, had been easily converted to this type of day-care facility. A large living room was comfortably furnished, and a dining room at one side provided three tables with a seating capacity of fourteen. Volunteers had recently built a wheelchair-access ramp to the front door as well as an accessible bathroom, thus enabling three other handicapped seniors to come.

According to the National Association of Adult Day Services, in 2002, more than thirty-five hundred adult day-care centers operated in the United States. These centers offer such diverse services that it is impossible to catalog them. Some centers provide little or no organized activities except daylong television watching, whereas other groups offer imaginative programs, such as tours, field trips, shopping expeditions, and special parties. Facilities range from a small converted garage or church basement to a new building staffed with nurses, physical therapists, and other health specialists.

Unlike a senior center, where residents make individual choices about recreation—be it a game, reading, listening to music, doing a puzzle, or just conversing with friends—a day-care center may offer a structured activities program. Many of the seniors require supervised or planned recreation, since they have some kind of behavioral, mental, or emotional disability.

Staffing depends on the size and financial capabilities of each center. A suggested staffing yardstick is a trained staff member for every six adults. In a small organization with a half-dozen clients, an administrator may be the only paid employee; all the aides are volunteers. The noon meal might be provided by a church organization eager for a money-making or service project.

In larger day-care centers, there may be salaried assistants and a cook, if meals are not catered. Recreational therapists, physical therapists, and gerontologists might also be on staff or serve as consultants.

In all cases, the administrator should have management and administrative abilities as well as some experience working with the aged. Training in occupational and recreational therapy provides an added plus.

Senior Citizen Centers

Gertrude Landau was thirty-two in 1943 when she established and directed the world's first senior center. Then a social worker, she volunteered to invite elderly people in the Bronx, New York, to use a room where they could drink coffee, play cards, and listen to the radio. Today, New York City has 340 senior centers serving some forty thousand men and women daily. Nationally there are more than fifteen thousand centers. Many have expanded their activities well beyond the social level by introducing language instruction, educational courses, counseling on health and finances, and advice on housing and legal problems, to name but a few. In many centers, the most important service is the midday hot meal.

Every senior citizen center is a busy place, for it provides many services for a community's elderly. Although no two have identical programs, the Crestwood Senior Center, located in a large southwestern town, provides an excellent example of what happens in the daily routine of one of these centers and the employment opportunities it may offer.

Marilyn Daley, the director, walked us through the facility. "We have a true center for our seniors who are not housebound," she said, as we walked into a large well-lit room, where a number of men and women sat at several card tables. Some were playing bridge, others played various games, and a handful huddled over jigsaw puzzles. "We have all kinds of tournaments for our regular patrons, and it's not unusual to find fifty to sixty people here on a morning or afternoon. From time to time, our programs include guest speakers and entertainers, teachers, artists, and musicians, men and women who are very generous in giving of themselves. I've discovered that all one needs do is to ask them, and they readily agree to come."

In an ell off the meeting room, an exhibition of watercolors was displayed. According to Marilyn, many seniors are quite artistic, and this room provides a good showcase for their art.

The dining area was a cheerful room with tables set for four and eight. "We serve a tasty, balanced noon meal every weekday," Marilyn said. "It's the best buy in town at a dollar and a quarter. Our chef prepares an average of seventy-five dinners each day for the dining room. No one goes hungry because we have a special fund to include those who cannot afford even that modest price."

The kitchen, with its stainless steel equipment and gleaming white walls, had the look of a modern restaurant. "Here's where we not only prepare the meals served in our dining room, but we also cook dinners for some fifty-five housebound elderly who participate in our 'meals on wheels' program.

"Volunteers—many of them husband-and-wife teams—deliver the food. They come here about eleven-thirty on weekdays and pick up the meals for the seniors on their routes."

"But what happens on Saturday and Sunday?"

"Nothing, because we're closed," Marilyn replied. "Everyone has to make other arrangements. It's too bad, but a limited budget restricts our operation to five days a week."

She led us on into her office, introduced us to her secretary and then to Alison Walker, the trained social worker. She explained that she is responsible for helping seniors solve the many problems that arise.

"For example," Alison said, "I assist those who are eligible to obtain food stamps, extra rent and fuel allowances, and bank loans, and offer other financial help. Coping with illness, health care planning, and legal issues, as well as explaining Medicare and Medicaid procedures and helping fill out insurance forms takes a lot of my time, too. We want our seniors to know they can bring their worries and problems to us, and we will do our best to help solve them."

Alison said that unlike cities where there are various government social service and welfare offices, in most small towns there might be no agency where the elderly can seek help. This has made it necessary for senior citizen centers to provide counseling and other assistance to individuals who otherwise have no place to turn. Elder abuse is a recurring problem as is the need for emotional counseling. "We're also a clearinghouse for information, but of course I don't have all the answers. I'm a good digger; if I don't have the answer, I'll find it!"

Next we peeked into the large garage attached to the center. "We're proud of these two vans." Marilyn beamed as she pointed to them. "We use them to pick up seniors from all over town and take them shopping twice a week. In addition, the vans transport people every day to and from the day-care center, and frequently they take men and women to special events."

In addition to Marilyn, the staff includes her secretary, who doubles as a bookkeeper, as well as the social worker, the chef and his four part-time assistants, and the two van drivers.

"None of us is getting rich," Marilyn explained, "but there is much joy as well as real personal satisfaction in providing these services, which we know are so greatly appreciated."

Apartments for Seniors

Many communities have some form of senior citizen housing that is open to low-income elderly persons who seek privacy but no longer can manage living in a home of their own. These facilities vary in size from one- or two-story garden-style buildings to high-rises, generally found in metropolitan areas. Some housing projects offer meals, housecleaning, transportation, wellness programs, and weekly outings.

Employment opportunities vary according to the type of apartments. In public projects, jobs may be limited to a superintendent and perhaps a secretary and/or an accountant, together with custodians and maintenance personnel who clean and make building repairs as well as care for the grounds. On the other hand, where services are provided, there is a broader job spectrum. In addition to the staff required in a public housing complex, jobs might include kitchen and dining room crews, a coordinator to arrange services, and other support personnel.

Inquire at the local senior center or your state human services division for the locations of housing for seniors.

Shared Housing

Shared housing involves a living arrangement where two or more unrelated people share a home. Many elderly people invite one or more senior friends to share their homes and pay part of the expenses, but larger groups have been organized by local shared housing associations or other community social services. There are more than 350 shared housing programs in forty-five states, with more in Canada and England. These programs help match home owners with home seekers and assist others in owning and operating shared group residences. They serve elders, students, displaced homemakers, single parents, and others who need reasonably priced housing or the services that are often part of such residences.

In larger homes, a live-in manager may be responsible for operating the facility. Residents may provide services in exchange for rent, but paid employees may be required in areas such as maintenance and housekeeping. Geriatric aides are employed in some homes.

If the concept intrigues you and you would like to see what is available in your area, you will need to visit the National Shared Housing Resource Center, which is currently available only online at www.nationalsharedhousing.org. This clearinghouse will direct you to a local center.

Solving Elder-Care Problems

Even back in the 1990s it was estimated that a company with one thousand employees that does not offer elder care would lose $400,000 annually because of the absenteeism of employee caregivers. It has also been estimated that 30 percent of all workers soon will have some type of elder-care responsibility.

Many companies have already recognized and taken steps to alleviate employee child-care problems, but comparatively few have done much to help personnel who are absent because they must care for elderly parents. Passage of the federal Family and Medical Leave Act (FMLA) forced larger businesses to address the elder-care problem. However, more than half of all Americans work for small companies that are exempt from the requirements of the FMLA.

Some companies have banded together to work out solutions, others have turned to existing community volunteer services, and some have instituted their own counseling services or forms of case management. Perhaps the largest cooperative partnership is the American Business Collaboration for Quality Dependent Care, which has funded more than fifteen hundred child-care and elder-care projects.

For more information about this collaboration and the broad variety of solutions to dependent-care issues, visit the website at www.abcdependentcare.com.

Long-Distance Love

Roger Benson, a West Coast carpenter, was concerned about his seventy-eight-year-old father, a widower who lived in Providence, Rhode Island. The senior Benson had been diagnosed with stage-one Alzheimer's disease. He was still able to function independently but subject to frequent memory loss and occasional wanderings. Not ready for nursing home care, he still asserted his independence, but Roger recognized that someone needed to check on his father daily and be available should he need help.

Delores DeSullas, a Detroit single mother of five, had a similar problem. Her mother, who lived alone in Atlanta, was in her eighties and refused to move into a senior citizen housing project or a shared living arrangement. Delores asked one of her mother's close neighbors if she would check on her mother, but the woman proved unreliable. Delores decided to search for someone who could stop in at least every other day. Where could she turn?

These are but two examples of a serious need that exists almost everywhere and is only now beginning to be addressed. It is anticipated that care for the elderly will become a larger problem than child care for most working people. Many single elderly men and women—and some couples, too—who live alone eventually need care or help of one kind or another. They may have no one to whom they can turn. The large baby boomer generation faces the problem of caring for parents, many of whom cannot afford to enter any kind of senior housing or supportive living home or who insist on living alone.

Eldercare Locator

Since 1991, the Eldercare Locator has helped families and friends find information about community services for older people anywhere in the United States and its territories. This is a collaborative project of the U.S. Administration on Aging, Inc., the National Association of State Units on Aging, and the National Association of Area Agencies on Aging.

Contacting a local agency makes sense. There are hundreds of new companies that provide case management or, in other words, monitor the affairs of aging relatives not living near their children or families. In one typical assignment, the company found a housekeeper to come twice a week to clean, shop, and take the client to appointments; arranged for delivery of a daily meal; directed a social worker to make certain all was running smoothly and, in the event of an emergency, to respond immediately. After a first consultation fee of $150, the company charged about $100 a month ($65 an hour). The housekeeper and meal provider were paid separately.

The geriatric case manager of another company took care of a ninety-three-year-old woman who fell, was hospitalized, moved to an assisted-living residence, was hospitalized again with pneumonia, and finally moved to a facility where she could receive twenty-four-hour care. Throughout all of this, the family, which lived several hundred miles away, was never involved except for consultation.

The opportunities to care for seniors in these situations are endless, and the need for care managers will grow. If you feel that you have the personality and experience to qualify for such a position, you may want to contact some of the companies in your area. To locate possible employers, call the Eldercare Locator or look in the Yellow Pages under "Social Services" for the name and phone number of the most appropriate agency to call for information. If the person you contact cannot help, he or she can refer you to the appropriate agency.

Caregiving on Your Own

If Eldercare Locator lists few or no such companies or services in your community, you might consider starting your own business. Services you might offer to prospective clients could include the following:

- Checking morning and night by phone or in person
- Taking clients for a ride, shopping, or to the doctor, dentist, hospital, hairdresser, and so forth
- Preparing meals or obtaining meals on wheels
- Housecleaning
- Walking the dog

- Obtaining the services and supervising the work of a plumber, painter, electrician, or other tradesperson for major or minor maintenance
- Being available twenty-four hours a day to respond to emergencies

You can promote your business by preparing a simple brochure describing what you do and leaving copies with local doctors, senior citizen centers, day-care centers, social workers, hospital discharge administrators, councils on the aging, and home health agencies. You might also try to obtain publicity in your local newspaper by writing a press release about your new business and the need for elder care in the community.

You will probably have to experiment with your fee schedule. Either work out a retainer fee for providing services needed on a regular basis (such as checking daily, cooking, cleaning, shopping) or charge on an hourly or per-visit basis.

For more information about this profession, you might investigate the National Association of Professional Geriatric Care Managers. It was founded in 1983 and had more than fourteen hundred members by 2002. These range from corporations to small home-based businesses whose clients are relatives who live some distance from the elder needing care. Most home-care businesses are owned and operated by nurses, social workers, or individuals who have adapted their knowledge and experience to providing a service they believe seniors in the community need.

For Further Information

Organizations

American Business Collaboration
200 Talcott Avenue West
Watertown, MA 02472
www.abcdependentcare.com

Eldercare Locator
National Association of Area Agencies on Aging
927 Fifteenth Street NW, Sixth Floor
Washington, DC 20005
www.eldercare.gov
www.n4a.org

Health Canada
Address Locator 0900C2
Ottawa, ON K1A 0K9
Canada
www.hc-sc.gc.ca/seniors-aines

National Association of Professional Geriatric Care Managers
1604 North Country Club Road
Tucson, AZ 85716
www.caremanager.org

CHAPTER SIX

Caregiving in Child Day-Care Centers

Child care is among the fastest-growing industries. With so many families forced to earn two incomes to meet their obligations as well as the increasing number of single-parent families, the potential for careers in child care can be appreciated. In one Harvard study, during a thirty-day period, 35 percent of female workers and 24 percent of male workers had to cut back hours at least one day out of seven to care for a family member. Business and industry have found this a challenging problem, especially for their personnel managers, who often must help employees locate child-care facilities.

Child care is not a new concept; Mrs. Joseph Hall established the first day nursery for children of seamen's widows and working wives in 1838. Fourteen years later, the Nurses' and Children's Hospital in New York City began to care for children of working women who had been patients of the institution.

The 1893 Chicago World's Fair featured a day nursery, which welcomed some ten thousand children. Five years after the fair closed, the National Federation of Day Nurseries listed 175 nursing operations, most of which operated in converted homes. Under the New Deal during the 1930s, the number swelled to more than nineteen hundred but fell off as federal financing was withdrawn. About 52 percent of all children have mothers that work. About 27 percent of preschoolers are cared for by nonrelatives; 16 percent are in preschools.

In 2000, it was estimated that there were some 120,000 day-care centers for children scattered across the nation. According to the *Occupational Outlook Handbook*, by the late 1990s, preschool teachers and child-care workers held about 1.3 million jobs.

Almost all day-care centers provide at least some informal learning experiences. Such programs are referred to as either "open" or "closed" programs. The former describes a structured plan, which provides for social development but no formal learning; the closed program offers the children daily procedures that emphasize the learning process more than social development or self-expression.

Child caregivers are known by various titles: baby-sitter, caretaker, child minder, teacher, day-care provider, or caregiver. Many older women, and a growing number of men, are found in the ranks. Applicants will find that educational and experience requirements vary widely from center to center. Some want teachers who have specialized in early childhood education; others only hire individuals who have a bachelor's degree; many seek applicants who have earned a C.D.A. (child development associate) degree at a junior college or two-year vocational-technical school. Former or working elementary school teachers usually find a welcome at many centers.

Positions at Child Day-Care Centers

People who manage small centers in their homes may need an untrained assistant or two. The staff of the typical large center is usually organized along the following lines:

Administrative Director

This individual is responsible for the overall administration of the organization and program planning. He or she may have a secretary and perhaps an assistant, in addition to the usual office support staff. Educational requirements range from a bachelor's degree in education plus two years' experience working with children to a master's degree in education.

Head Teacher

In this profession, caregivers are commonly called teachers because some emphasis is placed on learning. The head teacher is in charge of the teaching staff and is responsible for day-to-day planning and contact with parents. A high school diploma is the minimum educational requirement, but many centers want teachers who have earned a C.D.A. degree.

Teacher

The basic caregiving staff consists of teachers who might be expected to have an educational background similar to that of the head teacher.

Teacher's Aide

These individuals might be volunteers or paid employees who have qualifications similar to those expected of teachers.

Typical Child Day-Care Centers

There are a few basic types of day-care centers, all of which have a common purpose: to care for infants and/or young children of working parents who are unable to keep them at home during the day.

Nonprofit Day-Care Centers

Generally these are operated by churches, colleges, and universities, YMCAs, YWCAs, parent-run cooperatives, and a few businesses that provide emergency child care on-site.

Thousands of businesses have founded programs to help provide child care for employees. For the most part, these companies work with local community child-care agencies or organizations that the corporations support to provide community-wide solutions to these concerns. One joint venture is the American Business Collaboration for Quality Dependent Care, which was established in 1992 to help increase the supply and quality of care services. More than a hundred regional or local companies partner with twenty-one large corporations to launch specific initiatives that positively impact local communities. The initial two-year investment of $27 million helped finance hundreds of child- and elder-care projects across the United States. This effort created after-school and vacation programs for older children, as well as many new day-care centers for young children. During the second phase, 1995–2000, an additional $100 million was committed to solving dependent-care problems. Clearly a real opportunity exists for those who want to become involved in this activity.

Emergency Child Care

Corporate child care is a recent development, pioneered in 1986 by the Washington law firm of Wilmer, Cutler and Pickering. Other firms soon followed suit, and many large banks, financial institutions, and businesses have since followed their examples. All these firms realized that providing a child-care center for employee emergencies would help reduce absenteeism and spare their employees worry and trauma when regular caregivers were unable to come or their day-care centers were closed.

In most instances, high-quality care in inviting surroundings is offered. Trained staff and well-planned, imaginative programs are offered. Most businesses do not charge fees, but employees are usually limited in their use of the centers.

If you want to investigate possible job openings in your area, inquire at your local state employment security office, private employment agencies, or the personnel offices of large law firms and other companies.

Public Day-Care Centers

These child-care facilities are organized and operated by school districts, cities, towns, counties, and states or provinces. In some cases, they take the form of recreation programs run during vacations or special holiday periods. In a big city, hundreds of these government-sponsored facilities care for thousands of children.

Transit companies have realized that encouraging day-care centers to open near stations attracts riders. A $1.5 million child-care center was constructed near the Shady Grove station of the Washington Metropolitan Transit Authority. San Francisco's transit authority is urging developers to build day-care centers near its stations, while the New York Metropolitan Transportation Authority is studying child-care sites on its railroads.

Recreational Day-Care Centers

The Cannon Mountain Ski Area in New Hampshire placed the following advertisement in local newspapers: "Day-Care Workers/Day-Care Supervisor—Needed for the 2002–2003 ski season. Applicants must demonstrate ability to care for children and be creative with child-centered activities. Supervisor needs at least one year prior experience in a day-care facility and a high school education."

The need for day-care workers exists not only in ski areas but also in hotels and other facilities located in many popular resorts. Cruise ships that provide child care for their passengers offer opportunity for paid travel to interesting and faraway places. If a nearby country club does not offer child care to its membership, you might consider proposing that you operate such a service for the membership.

Private Day-Care Centers

Most private day-care centers are run by individuals in their homes or rented quarters. They may accept as few as two or three children. Some parents who care for their own children at home consider this a good way to earn extra money. Some private day-care centers are much larger, however, with staffs of trained teachers and caregivers.

KinderCare Learning Centers has become the largest business organization providing child care. In 2002, the company operated some 1,250 centers serving more than 120,000 children. This company employs more than 27,000 people. "Teachers" must take a twelve-hour paid training course. This enables them to become familiar with the company's teaching methods and other aspects of the business, as well as deal effectively with parents.

The company is on the move, having opened its first commuter center in Lombard, Illinois, across from the Metra train station, making it convenient for working mothers and fathers to leave and pick up their children. Plans call for opening similar centers in other locations around the country. KinderCare now offers "Kids' Choice" centers for children age six and up. The company is expanding to large corporate centers, as well as overseas to Great Britain.

....

A Typical Midsize Day-Care Center

Many child-care centers operated by individuals accept a dozen or more children and require a modest capital investment, plus two or more full- or part-time teachers. The Elfin Children's Center described below might be considered typical.

The Elfin Children's Center is located downtown in a small eastern city. The center, formerly a large meeting hall, is an attractive room decorated in bright colors, furnished with tables and chairs suitable for small children, a sandbox, and various clusters of toys. The day we visited, some thirty preschool boys and girls soon came running, hopping, and skipping through the door, transforming the quiet into a joyous bedlam. The five teachers helped remove hats, gloves, and coats, which each child hung on his or her hook in the lobby. This freed the children to romp around the room until, on command, each went to one of the five teachers and quietly sat at a table. The day began with a story to encourage relaxation and gradual adjustment to the structured program.

A free-choice period followed the story. The children could play with toys, climb into the sandbox, or look at books. A group morning meeting came next, built around participation in simple crafts. Next, the teachers served midmorning snacks of milk and crackers.

Weather permitting, everyone then went outside for recreation and a learning activity, after which the whole school returned indoors to join in a singing session led by a local musician. Another free period preceded lunch, after which most of the children returned home in carpools. A few newcomers joined those who remained for the afternoon session.

The afternoon session began with an outdoor period of organized games, after which the teachers led the boys and girls back indoors for a two-hour rest period. Two newly arrived public school teachers kept the children busy until 5:30 P.M., when parents started arriving to take their little ones home. The elementary school teachers stayed until the last child called good-bye, then they put away the toys and craft articles and tidied up the room.

Patricia Gowan, who started the center, has a B.A. with a major in education and is enrolled in graduate school, taking night courses toward a master's degree. Her staff consists of three college graduates with bachelor's degrees in child development, child education, and elementary school education; two untrained aides who worked under the direction of the teachers; and two part-time elementary teachers from a nearby school.

Seventy children are enrolled in the program, the majority coming on Monday, Wednesday, and Friday and a few on Tuesday and Thursday for the morning session. A half-dozen, whose mothers worked, attend every day for both sessions. The fees generate sufficient revenue to pay the rent, insurance, staff salaries, and miscellaneous expenses, as well as provide Patricia an adequate income.

A Home-Based Day-Care Center

If you love children and want to take care of a few in your home, you can earn a modest income, depending on where you live and what you charge for your services.

Tamara Simmons lives in a small Midwest college town. After nearly completing her teaching degree, Tamara found she needed to stay home for a while to care for her baby. From the time her son was six months old, she has operated a state-licensed day-care center out of her home. The agency that licenses such an operation required forty hours of early childhood education classes, a health check, three references, and criminal disclosure. A state inspector checked her house for a whole list of requirements including smoke detectors, child gates, and outlet covers.

Because Tamara already had the extra ten educational hours needed for infant/toddler care, she can offer her services to any age child. The number of children allowed in home day care varies in her state, according to the number of children in a given age category. The maximum number ever allowed would be eight.

After some experimenting, Tamara set her weekly fees at $100 per week for full-time Monday through Friday care, and $65 per week for part-timers. By the day she charges $20 for a full day or $15 for a part day. Her hours are long—7:30 A.M. to 6:30 P.M. This past year she had a steady group of four children—a one-year-old baby, a two-year-old, and a seven- and ten-year-old in the after-school hours.

Tamara realized an estimated gross income for 2001 of $16,855. Her expenses included $1,500 for toys and art supplies. Tamara's state offers a reimbursement program for food, so although she paid $3,000 for meals and snacks, after she was reimbursed through the state, she ended up with only $650 in food expense. After all expenses, she realized a profit of only $7,000. However, Tamara finds the career enjoyable, and being able to care for her son at home is worth the work.

Each state has different regulations, and each community different needs. Find out from nearby home centers what you must do to start a center in your house and what your earning possibilities might be. If you decide to start your own center, you might want to remember Tamara's advice for everyone going into this business: "Always collect from parents at least a week in advance."

For Further Information

Organizations

KinderCare Learning Centers
650 Northeast Holladay Street, Suite 1400
Portland, OR 97232
www.kindercare.com

Career seekers in Canada will find much information from these two organizations:

The Canadian Child Care Federation
201–283 Parkdale Avenue
Ottawa, ON K1Y 4R4
Canada
www.cccf.fcsge.ca

The Council of Canadian Child and Youth Care Association
www.cyccanada.ca

Suggested Reading

Eberts, Marjorie, and Margaret Gisler. *Careers in Child Care.* Chicago: VGM Career Books, 2000.

Sciarra, Dorothy J., and Anne G. Dorsey. *Owning and Operating a Successful Child Care Center.* Delner Learning, 2002.

Wittenberg, Renee. *Opportunities in Child Care Careers.* Chicago: VGM Career Books, 1996.

CHAPTER SEVEN

Caregiving in Hospices

I n a southern California suburb, Mary Parker sat in Mercy Hospital at the bedside of a cancer patient on the final journey of his life. The patient's wife, who had been with the dying man all through the night, had gone home for a few hours' sleep. At the same time, Ellen Harkness, a registered nurse, was in the home of an elderly woman, checking her vital signs and making certain she was not in pain. Both caregivers were working for a hospice, Mary as a hospice volunteer and Ellen as a paid hospice nurse.

Webster defines *hospice* as "a homelike facility to provide supportive care for terminally ill patients." It is also defined as a "place of shelter for travelers, especially such a shelter maintained by monks." Today's hospice movement had its start during 1967 in Lydenham, England, when St. Christopher's Hospice opened. This was the inspiration of the dedicated Dame Cecily Saunders, an English hospice physician, who founded the current movement to provide a safe haven for the dying. In adopting the word *hospice*, she wanted to combine modern medical techniques with the kind of spiritual care the medieval religious orders made available to passing pilgrims.

The following brief excerpt from Larry Beresford's *The Hospice Handbook* describes the hospice movement as it exists presently:

The people who founded the modern hospice movement of humane care for the dying were guided by a few simple ideas. First, they believed that dying is a uniquely important time in a person's life. They viewed dying as the final stage of human existence and as a normal and natural process. But they also recognized that while death may be a natural process, it is rarely easy or simple. Hospice founders wanted to offer a specialized kind of support centered on the challenges unique to this process. They believed that care for the dying should involve a different set of skills than other kinds of health care, with primary emphasis on physical comfort and emotional support. They also believed that dying patients deserve to be informed about their medical condition and treatment alternatives, so they make meaningful choices about how to live in their remaining time and receive adequate care without having to feel demeaned.

Another observation of hospice founders was that the medical system frequently did not deal very well with the special needs of dying patients. . . .

Hospitals or other health facilities emphasize restoring health, not providing room, board, and minimal care for dying men, women, and children. Insurance companies and Medicaid and Medicare regulations pressure hospitals to discharge all patients in the shortest possible time, and most of the terminally ill do not qualify for Medicare payments as they lie in a hospital bed awaiting death. Generally speaking, hospice care is intended to be provided in the home, to augment the family's caregiving efforts, not to replace them.

In the United States, almost thirty years after Connecticut Hospice admitted its first patient in New Haven in 1974, hospices have spread to every state. The Hospice Association of America reports that its organization now represents more than twenty-eight hundred institutions serving hundreds of thousands of Americans each year, making this a significant part of the health field. Now, in many places, it is possible to die with dignity and without pain either at home or in a hospice with one's family nearby. Those who manage hospices believe that pain is unnecessary and that it is acceptable to administer as much morphine as needed to keep patients comfortable. They ignore the usual objection that morphine is addictive in view of the short life expectancy for these patients.

A HOSPICE PROGRAM'S PURPOSE

This is how the Hospice of the Upper Valley in Lebanon, New Hampshire, describes its purpose and program:

"Our purpose at Hospice of the Upper Valley is to care for people with life-threatening illnesses and their families. We have been doing this work since 1979. Our hospice is not a place, but a philosophy—a program of care that can be carried out in any setting. Our dedicated volunteers have been intensively trained to help patients and families through the crises of illness, death, and grief. We also offer extensive educational services to the community.

"Our work is carried out by trained volunteers who visit patients and families at home or in the hospital or nursing home. Assigned to one patient at a time, each volunteer is there when needed to provide emotional support as well as practical help to patients, family members, and friends.

"The volunteer service given to a patient or family may be as simple as preparing a meal, sitting and talking, picking up children from school, helping with transportation to medical appointments, or listening to a variety of questions and concerns. One of the most common requests is for companionship for the patient so that the primary caregiver can take a break, go to work, or do some shopping. We also provide coordination with other health-care services and are happy to attend medical appointments with the patient. We are available twenty-four hours a day, seven days a week. Help for hospice patients and their families is just a phone call away."

The tragic need for providing hospice services to persons afflicted with AIDS is growing. The Visiting Nurses and Hospice of San Francisco has found that 80 percent of its AIDS patients can die at home rather than in institutions.

Types of Hospices

- **Community-based hospices** are nonprofit groups governed by a board of trustees whose aim is to care for the community's hospice needs.
- **Hospital or nursing home hospices** may consist of a few rooms or a wing used exclusively for hospice purposes.
- **Home health agency hospices** assume hospice responsibilities that are offered in patients' homes.
- **Volunteer-based hospices** are independent groups that are usually found in rural communities where there are no health facilities. These organizations are limited to providing volunteers to visit in patients' homes.
- **Free-standing hospices** are separate from the hospital or nursing home but are associated with it.
- **Residential-based hospices** are independent organizations providing terminal care for patients who have no homes or cannot be cared for by families or friends.

In addition to the above, all of which are nonprofit, there are some privately owned hospices, one of the largest of which is VITAS Innovative Hospice Care, based in Miami, Florida, and operating in three states.

The Hospice Staff

Every hospice has an administrator, either volunteer or paid, to oversee the group's activities and direct its volunteer caregivers.

Depending on the organization's size and financial resources, there may be one or more staff members providing the usual office and building maintenance services, in addition to the professional staff members who provide the necessary social, economic, spiritual, and medical help that patients require.

The **registered nurse** (RN) is the medical case manager in most hospices. He or she is the contact between the doctor and patient and coordinates all the services of the other professional support members and the volunteer caregivers. A registered nurse usually visits each patient at least once a week and may be available on a twenty-four-hour basis.

A **personal care aide** is responsible for the total care of the patient, including bathing, grooming, hair and skin care, turning and repositioning in bed, as well as some housekeeping and even shopping chores. The aide may visit two hours once, twice, or three times a week, depending on the need. This individual is the key member of the hospice team for the patient, because it is he or she who is in an intimate relationship and can provide emotional support.

The **social worker** advises the family on financial matters, psychological problems, and obtaining other specialized assistance.

The **hospice chaplain** is an important member of the team, available to provide such spiritual comfort and support as the patient and the family may need. In some instances, this can be an essential service for the terminally ill, especially for those individuals who are not prepared to face death.

The **patient caregiver volunteer**, according to the Hospice of the Littleton Area in New Hampshire, "visits patients and their families at home, in the hospital, or in the nursing home. Volunteers provide help with routine tasks, give friendship, guidance, and support throughout the illness and bereavement. Examples of services include such things as preparing meals, helping with household chores, talking, picking up children at school, running errands, helping with transportation to medical appointments, or listening to a variety of questions and concerns. Volunteers can also provide a respite for family members by offering them the opportunity to go out for a few hours to shop, do errands, or relax."

This is not all. Hospice service does not end with the patient's death. In Littleton, a support group for persons dealing with grief and bereavement meets two nights a month with various qualified leaders. The group's literature explains its open-ended welcome: "You are free to come when you want and move on when you no longer need the support. Confidentiality will be respected."

Getting Involved as a Volunteer

If this career possibility interests you, consider joining a hospice group as a volunteer to learn firsthand about hospice care before you apply for a paid position in a hospice. Holly Lakey, director of the Hospice of the Littleton Area, seeks specific skills and qualifications in a volunteer.

"I want prospective volunteers to know something of our philosophy and program care. Essentially, I trust that a volunteer will have a caring heart, a helping hand, and a listening ear. Compassion and empathy are also important, as well as an ability to bring a supportive and caring presence into the hearts and homes of hospice friends. In addition, we seek individuals who have the ability to listen, to develop rapport and trust, to function in a team, and to bring sensitivity and maturity to the patient. Being responsible and dependable is most important.

"We achieve this through an eight-week training program for volunteers. Each meeting lasts two hours, and the subjects we cover include: Introduction and Expectations; Physical and Psychological Problems of the Terminally Ill; Spiritual Needs; Personal Death Acceptance; Pain Management; Personal Styles of Grieving; Communication Skills/Active Listening; Planning for Death; and Role of the Hospice Volunteer. All of the meetings are conducted by specialists in that field."

Holly explained that for volunteers who want to become involved in a hospice but do not feel capable of performing patient care, there are many other ways to help, including clerical and secretarial tasks; fund-raising; assisting in the preparation of the newsletter; public speaking to civic, church, and other community groups; participating in public relations and education programs in the community; serving on the board of directors or board committees; and undertaking special projects.

Opportunities with Hospice Organizations

With approximately twenty-eight hundred hospices in the United States and an average of only fifty-six to a state, hospice care may not seem the most promising field for those seeking a career. That should not discourage you, however, because as the following report on the small state of New Hampshire shows, there are opportunities, and there will be more as the movement expands.

During the early part of this decade, in the Granite State (population nearly 1.3 million), there were more than fifteen hospices ranging from small organizations with a single volunteer or paid director to large metropolitan hospices. Five groups reported on their budgets: one indicated $3 million to $7 million; two said $1 million to $3 million; and two reported $500,000 to $1 million. The number of services offered varied greatly; obviously, those with the largest budgets had the most extensive programs.

Hospices may lack the glamour of many other health agencies, but they ask those who enter this very special caring work to join a program that is distinguished from all other health care by its unique relationship, always ending in death. The opportunities for serving others during a time of extreme hardship are not to be found anywhere else in the caregiving profession. Whether you eventually work in an administrative or hospice professional position or as a volunteer, you will be a member of an exceptional group of dedicated men and women. You will have joined a movement which, though in its infancy, is bound to grow as our population ages. Volunteers and paid professionals alike have said that the principal reasons they wanted to become involved with hospice were a desire to give, to nurture, and to make a difference. Most of these men and women find this a positive experience because hospice patients share their inner strength and ability to focus on life while dealing with a life-threatening illness. As one woman said, "I feel I give so little and receive so much in return from the patient—gifts of sharing, strength, and beauty."

For Further Information

Organizations

American Hospice Foundation
2120 L Street NW
Washington, DC 20037
www.americanhospice.org

Hospice Association of America
228 Seventh Street SE
Washington, DC 20003
www.hospice-america.org

National Hospice and Palliative Care Organization
1700 Diagonal Road, Suite 625
Alexandria, VA 22314
www.nhcpo.org

National Hospice Organization
1901 North Moore Street, Suite 901
Arlington, VA 22209
www.nho.org

National Institute for Jewish Hospice
8723 Alden Drive
Los Angeles, CA 90048

Children's Hospice International
2202 Mount Vernon Avenue, Suite 3C
Alexandria, VA 22301
www.chionline.org

CHAPTER EIGHT

Caregiving in Home Health Services

I t happened suddenly, on the golf course: Joel Paxson, a recently retired energetic sixty-six-year-old golfer, felt an incredible pain hit the left side of his head. Joel had had a stroke. His companions rushed him to the hospital, where he was placed in intensive care with wires, tubes, monitoring machines, and anxious nurses.

A few days later, Susan, his wife, was called to the patient services office. The discharge clerk told her that the hospital was discharging Joel the next day.

"But I'm all alone!" Susan protested. Her husband was paralyzed on the left side and unable to speak. "How can I take care of him? He'll need help for everything from eating to dressing to physical therapy. I can't handle it." She knew their modest savings would not last long if he went to a nursing home at $3,000 or more a month. She was devastated.

"There is a wonderful solution, and I have set it up for you," the clerk told her. "The home health care agency will send a homemaker, aides, a physical therapist, and a registered nurse. In addition, they will prepare a plan for helping you cope—it's called managed care and will include assisting your husband in his recovery. Furthermore, Medicare will pay for all of his expenses."

Our home health organizations are at the forefront of the battle to achieve better health care at less cost. A natural growth from the former visiting nurse associations—which, as the name implies, confined their activities to nursing services—today's home health organizations have become one of the basic health providers, a growing $36 billion industry. With the reduction in the number of days a patient may stay in the hospital and techno- logical advances that reduce the average patient stay, the trend toward increased home care services will continue to rise. In fact, home health care is expected to become the fastest-growing seg- ment of our health industry. It has come a long way from the days when nurses visited the sick in their homes. Today, the home health care provider can literally bring the hospital into the home as technicians install life-saving devices and other equipment at the patient's bedside in his or her familiar bedroom.

Three broad types of organizations provide home health care:

1. The traditional visiting nurse associations, most of which have broadened their functions and become known as home health agencies. Almost all are community based and nonprofit.
2. For-profit and nonprofit private organizations, as well as a number of hospitals and nursing homes that offer some or all of the services as the agencies mentioned above.
3. Individual entrepreneurs or contractors who offer specialized or a limited number of services.

Attitudes Toward Home Health Services

Before we describe the activities of home health care providers in more detail, let's take a quick look to see what the patients or pub- lic think about this segment of the health industry.

Olsten Healthcare (a home health organization) conducted a survey in 1993 to learn the extent of health care usage—how peo- ple view their experiences with home health care services—and to explore policy issues, such as the role home health care should play in a national health plan.

With Olsten Healthcare's permission, we quote briefly from the report's summary to show the high esteem in which the public regards these important caregivers:

"Home health care services should be encouraged to help reduce the cost of health care in this country... fully 97 percent of those experienced with home care agree with this premise. Most (77 percent) agree strongly, while another 20 percent agree, though less strenuously.

"Overall, 94 percent of experienced people are satisfied with the services that have been delivered, with 61 percent extremely satisfied.

"Satisfaction is so prevalent that virtually all experienced people would recommend home health care services to their families and friends (97 percent).

"Moreover, perceptions about the cost of home health care services are quite favorable. Most believe the cost of treatment in the home is lower than it would be in a hospital setting or other long-term facility (90 percent).

"Nearly as many agree that home healthcare services are an 'affordable' alternative to hospitalization or long-term nursing home care (88 percent)."

Everyone considering a career in a home health organization should be encouraged by the public perception of this growing segment of the health industry.

Medical Devices Come Home

One of the most exciting developments in home care is the gradual introduction of medical devices used in patients' residences. Once it was necessary for a patient to remain in a hospital as long as the use of a ventilator, a catheter, oxygen, infusion pump, or blood glucose monitor was required. However, with the pressure to shorten hospital stays and the availability of trained nurses and technicians who go into the home, a revolution is taking place in health care delivery. Patients who can return home usually recover faster and are happier in their familiar family surroundings. Equally important to many patients is the cost saving of home health care.

Many job opportunities exist involving home medical equipment. According to a special committee report issued by the U.S. Center for Devices and Radiological Health: "Medical devices used in the home are often very sophisticated and require skilled operators to maintain them effectively and safely. If a patient must hire outside help for home health care, it is imperative that this care is provided by medical and health personnel who are trained to use medical devices. The most likely source of this care would be an accredited home health agency or home medical equipment supply company whose employees have been examined and deemed qualified to provide skilled services."

Regarding certification of homemaker/home health aides, the report states: "Nationally mandated certification standards for this type of caregiver went into effect on August 14, 1990. These home health care providers must meet minimum standards and be judged competent to provide designated services anywhere in the United States. Aides will be prohibited from performing services until they have completed training and demonstrated competence. Agencies must also provide in-service training to ensure continued competence."

This committee report indicates the extent of the home health agency's responsibilities and gives interested readers an idea of the career possibilities in this field, especially those who contemplate becoming aides. Career possibilities also exist with supply companies that provide the home medical equipment used in home health care as well as in hospitals and nursing homes. Their trained employees not only deliver the equipment but also set it up and instruct the caregivers in the use of the devices.

Case Management

The average patient who receives home health services does not realize the amount of planning, scheduling, record keeping, and work that is required to deliver efficient and often lifesaving health care. *Case management* is the term commonly applied to this key to the success of a home health care agency or organization.

Quoting from the U.S. Center for Devices and Radiological Health's special committee report, case management has been defined as consisting of "patient and family services to ensure the patient's safety and supply of goods and services through an individualized home health care plan. This plan provides health assessment; facilitates access to appropriate, cost-effective services and equipment; and maximizes patients' functional independence to prevent insufficient, inadequate, excessive, or fragmented services and unsafe conditions."

According to the report, it is the case manager who assesses the patient, the prospective caregivers, and the home environment to ascertain whether safe and effective device-related home health care is in place. The case manager identifies needs for intermittent treatment, education, intervention, and interaction by care providers and technicians. The case manager discusses patient care needs with the physician and other relevant caregivers and makes the appropriate contacts for medical services and equipment on behalf of the patient. All of these assessments, physician conferences, contacts with caregivers, and equipment arrangements are documented in the patient record.

The report also calls for both the patient and the family to learn how to use the highly complex technological devices. This is often done under extremely stressful conditions, because failure to learn to use the devices safely and effectively can have drastic results. In a hospital setting, backup systems and experts are on the scene twenty-four hours a day, with personnel ready to handle emergencies and to operate and repair machines, generators to supply backup power during outages, and a nursing staff to provide oversight. At home, all of these responsibilities rest on the shoulders of the patient and the family with only intermittent professional supervision. The professionals who provide home health care are therefore essential to the entire process.

....

Home Health Agencies

A typical home health agency (HHA) might best be described as an organization that services a definite geographical area comprising a few or dozens of communities and that operates a system for delivering health care to patients' homes. Employees of these agencies work in either the administrative section, which is responsible for running the show behind the scenes, or the professional and subprofessional staff—those men and women who deliver the care and work directly with the patients and the public.

The staff of one typical HHA, serving some twenty-five communities, consists of the following personnel (the numerals following each title indicate the number of employees working in that category).

ADMINISTRATIVE
Administrator (1)
Office staff (4)
Supervisory staff (5)
Program coordinator (1)

PROFESSIONAL AND SUBPROFESSIONAL CAREGIVERS
RN staff (13)
LPN staff (2)
Occupational therapist (1)
Physical therapists (5)
Speech therapists (2)
Social workers (2)

Homemaker/home health aides (25)
Adult in-home care providers (26)
Homemakers (2)

Brief job descriptions of the professional caregivers in this list appear in Chapter 3, with the exception of program coordinator, home health aides, in-home care providers, and homemakers, which are covered here.

The **program coordinator** is responsible for program development, quality care assurance, and coordinating learning programs for the staff.

A **homemaker/home health aide** is a certified, licensed individual trained to perform duties that are unique to the position and essential to patient care. In addition to bathing, dressing, and grooming; providing mouth, skin, and nail care; and applying uncomplicated dressings, the aide may help plan diets, prepare meals, and perform household tasks essential to the patients' health, as well as provide emotional care and respite, as needed.

An **adult in-home care provider** may work for as few as one or two hours a week or as many as thirty-five or forty, depending on the needs of the patient to whom he or she is assigned and the HHA's patient load. In-home care providers help patients who may need assistance with certain daily living activities but do not require skilled nursing care or help from aides. Essentially, they are companions to those living alone and respite for caregivers who need to get out of the house. Generally they may help with planning and preparing meals, doing light housekeeping and laundry, changing beds, and running errands.

A **homemaker** performs light housekeeping, meal preparation, and laundry. He or she does what is needed and then leaves. Homemakers cannot touch the patients (who must be able to walk and care for themselves) and are not expected to be companions.

Many HHAs are becoming involved with local hospice organizations (see Chapter 7) and provide the necessary health professionals to aid those patients who have entered hospice or are receiving it in their homes.

Since the HHA is a system of delivering health care to patients' homes, there is necessarily a great deal of travel required of the caregivers. In mountainous or northern climates, this can occasionally require driving during periods of hazardous road conditions; in warm climates, there may be other problems such as excessive heat and dangerous turbulent weather problems.

Other Home Health Services

Private Health Service Companies

The Calldoctor Company is an example of a specialized and sophisticated type of entrepreneurial company that provides services not normally offered by the usual HHA. This company, based in San Diego, has a fleet of specially designed vans marked with a catchy toll-free number. It staffs each with a doctor and a technician trained to handle many problems that would usually require a trip to a physician or hospital. The company reports having made more than sixty thousand house calls in three counties to date.

The vans contain much of the same equipment found in a hospital emergency room, including an x-ray machine. Calldoctor enables a patient to avoid a more expensive trip to a hospital, but if the doctor decides that hospitalization is needed, he phones ahead to the facility so that the patient can be admitted promptly.

Another organization, located in a Boston suburb, specializes in treating people who have been severely disabled because of an injury or illness. Here we find a professional team drawn from a pool of physicians, nurses, occupational and physical therapists, and social workers. Bringing the professional to the patient makes life a little easier for those whose mobility has become extremely limited.

The HHA is often called on by private companies, too, when it comes to home-infusion services, which provide at-home patients with painkillers, antibiotics, intravenous nutritional supplements, and anticancer drugs, all under the direction of expert nurses or technicians who work for an HHA.

Nurses' Registries

Finding nurses (RNs and LPNs as well as Nurse's Aides) can be a nightmare for the person who suddenly needs assistance for an injured or sick relative or friend. While some professionals' names may appear in the Yellow Pages and a local HHA may compile a roster of nurses, such lists are of limited value because this information gets out-of-date, and nurses whose names appear on the list may be working.

Therefore, a nurses' registry or clearinghouse can provide a much-needed service because it has a sufficient number of registered individuals to fill quickly each order it receives. It sends out only reliable nurses whose references have been carefully checked. In small communities, there would probably not be sufficient call for such a service nor enough nurses to provide the necessary backlog. However, in cities and large towns, this could prove a profitable and very much-needed service.

If this interests you, investigate the need for a registry by talking with the head nurses and the discharge planners at hospitals, nursing home administrators, the local HHA, other home health providers, and the local state employment security office. You may have to obtain a permit from the state, county, or municipal agency that licenses employment agencies.

Starting and running such a business would require many tasks, including:

- Find and sign up nurses willing to be listed with you
- Do a reference check on each
- Advertise and promote your agency

- Collect money due from clients who retain your services
- Pay the nurses
- Do the accounting
- Check constantly on nurse availability and be prepared to offer twenty-four-hour service

Most agencies add a percentage to the going hourly rate for each type of nurse, to cover overhead and profit. It might be feasible to expand your registry to include other types of health workers, equipment, and services.

The Outlook for Home Health Care

With hospitals discharging patients sooner, the cost of institutional care mounting, and the reluctance of the average person to seek hospital care, the demand for home care services will continue to rise. This will create a wide range of issues for the average HHA. It will require the administrative staff of each HHA to carefully plan the future, considering such issues as staffing needs (administrative, professional, nursing), additional space, training requirements, financing, and many other factors. All this points to a challenging and promising future for those who choose to pursue a career in this segment of health care.

For Further Information

Organizations

American Network of Home Health Care Social Workers, Inc.
1187 Wilmette Avenue, Number 139
Wilmette, IL 60091
www.homehealthsocialwork.org

The Care Guide
9 Cedarview Drive
West Hill, ON M1C 2K5
Canada
www.thecareguide.com

The Division of Aging and Seniors
Health Canada
Address Locator 190841
Ottawa, ON K1A 1B4
Canada

Elder Care Home Health
www.eldercarehomehealth.com

National Association for Home Care
228 Seventh Street SE
Washington, DC 20003
www.nahc.org

CHAPTER NINE

Caregiving in Social Services

" 'm a failure," the middle-aged man said, looking away from the social worker who sat across from him in a family agency office. "I don't know why I came," Mr. Benson continued. "There's nothing you can do for me."

Mr. Benson had lost his job as a meat cutter when the packing plant where he worked closed. That very same day, the doctor told his wife that she required a serious and expensive operation. Little wonder he was upset and discouraged.

"I am sure we can help you." The social worker's voice was so calm and reassuring that Mr. Benson turned toward him. For the first time in days, his face broke into a faint smile. After several more days, the social worker had helped Mr. Benson take an inventory of his job skills, and, with new confidence, he was able to find a position where his experience and abilities were needed. Meanwhile, the social worker arranged for the financing of the operation.

This case is typical of how a social worker helps people individually and in family units. Casework is the very core of social work—although by no means all of it. The principal method by which social agencies help others is through social casework. This is the only way that an agency representative can become acquainted with the problems of the individual or family unit and learn all the necessary facts that enable him or her to recommend or take necessary corrective action. Assigning a caseworker to a problem is expensive, but it is the only way to complete the job thoroughly.

Actually, increasing numbers of social workers are also working with groups of children, youth, parents, hospital patients, addicts, and others when it would be impractical to treat such people individually.

The relatively new profession of social work has matured from charitable associations providing assistance to the poor to a discipline that uses scientific methods, creativity, and compassion to respond to a wide variety of social problems. Social workers help families who face economic hardships or emotional challenges. They work within communities to support welfare programs. They work in hospitals and schools and nursing homes and juvenile justice systems.

Social workers earn their credentials through completing at least a two-year postgraduate program and earning a master's or doctorate degree in social work. Many social workers complete clinical internships before being certified or licensed.

Defining Social Work

You will find as many definitions of the term *social work* as there are workers in the field. Social work means helping people who are in need, people who may require money, medical attention, psychiatric assistance, vocational guidance, family counseling, or other special services that will help them conquer their troubles. This assistance is delivered by social workers—men and women who are professionally trained and highly skilled in the field.

Social work is essentially a helping profession, assisting those who have problems, to enable them to realize happy and satisfying lives. Like medicine, nursing, or the ministry, social work can bring great personal rewards.

Personal Qualifications

To be successful in social work, it is not enough to like, understand, and want to help people. Other personal traits and aptitudes are necessary, too. The principal ones include:

- Ability to read with comprehension and express yourself clearly in writing and speech
- Desire to apply ideas and imagination to your work each day
- Perseverance to complete whatever you undertake, no matter how difficult the task
- Ability to take directions and work with others as a member of a team
- Curiosity to discover the causes of human or social problems or difficulties you encounter
- Cheerfulness to carry you through unhappy or unpleasant work experiences
- Interest in reading and learning, because social workers are constantly seeking more knowledge and better ways of doing the job
- Tolerance to work with a range of people with interests and perspectives different from your own
- Insight to determine your inner strengths and weaknesses plus willpower that is strong enough to make you correct your deficiencies

A Statewide Social Service Organization

To give you an idea of how one statewide organization serves the needs of families and children, the following is a list of the programs it offers:

- Adult home care, homemaker, and respite programs
- Pregnancy counseling, infant foster care, adoption and search, and family crisis intervention programs
- Family counseling program with after-hours clinic
- Advocacy program
- Teens program (runaway and homeless youth, drug abuse, and transitional living)
- Family sponsor, parenting plus, and parent-aide program
- Group home-education program

In addition to the directors of each of the above programs, there are trained and volunteer staff members, the executive director, treasurer, director of development, office manager, and clerical support personnel. Financial support comes from fees, grants, state aid, and contributions.

Typical Jobs in Social Work

There are many different job titles in social work, and different agencies may give identical jobs different names or responsibilities. However, to give some indication of the wide scope of job responsibilities in the social work field, a sampling of typical jobs in which you will find openings after obtaining the training and experience required by each are listed below. There are many more positions than those listed here.

For example, within group work, positions include group workers, supervisors, program directors, consultants, and department heads in charge of group work. There are many kinds of group work, including working with children, with the aged, in hospitals and clinics, in camps, in community and recreation centers, in correctional institutions, in churches and youth organizations, and in housing developments. For all of the jobs listed here, you need special training in social work, with the exception of fund-raising and public-relations directors and support staff.

- **Administrator** (of a social service or public welfare agency): the individual who holds this title is the top executive of an agency or institution. He or she is responsible for all planning, handling of finances, and directing the entire operation (generally with the aid of a staff).
- **Administrative assistant:** acts as an assistant to an administrator or other top executive. He or she performs various assignments and, in the superior's absence, may assume his or her duties and responsibilities.
- **Case consultant:** an experienced caseworker or social worker who counsels other social workers as well as those laypeople and professionals who are involved in some aspect of social work but have no training in the field.
- **Caseworker:** a trained social worker who investigates cases of personal and family maladjustment and need and gives advice and assistance.
- **Community organization worker:** a social worker who specializes in helping various agencies in a community work together more effectively.
- **Department head:** the executive who directs all of the activities of a single department within an organization and is responsible for everything done within that unit.
- **Director of fund-raising:** an executive who organizes and supervises all aspects of a campaign to solicit funds for an organization.
- **Director of public relations:** in charge of a public relations department or responsible for the public relations function of an organization.
- **Field supervisor:** a staff member of a social service agency or a university professor to whom a student reports while obtaining training in the field—such as a social service agency—as part of postgraduate study in social work.
- **Group worker:** a social worker who specializes in working with groups of people rather than with individuals.

- **Research assistant**: obtains basic data and information and does preliminary analytical work under the direction of a supervisor.
- **Research director**: a social worker who plans and administers all of the work of a research staff that collects, analyzes, and interprets data for a government or private social work agency.
- **Support staff**: consists of one or more of the following employees: office manager, personnel manager, research specialist, secretary, computer operator, file clerk, mail clerk, and receptionist/switchboard operator. Although few of these positions are involved with the agency's clients, they are an essential part of the team and share in the overall goal of striving for effective results. If you have acquired the necessary skills to qualify for one of these jobs, you should be able to fit into the agency's work pattern without any difficulty.

An Overview of Casework

Some of the most involved and time-consuming cases are those handled by caseworkers in public welfare agencies, responsible for making allotments of public funds. These social workers have a triple responsibility—prudent handling of the taxpayers' money, wise counseling, and provision of adequate relief funds to each needy client who applies for help.

Other caseworker responsibilities include:

- Helping individuals, families, and the aged with every kind of personal problem and securing financial aid as well as health care and other services needed
- Counseling the blind or disabled
- Placing children in foster homes or arranging for their adoptions

- Working in medical or psychiatric clinics and hospitals as a member of a rehabilitation team
- Serving on the staff of child care and adoption agencies, child guidance clinics, churches, correctional and protective institutions, family service agencies, hospitals, military establishments, programs for the aged, public welfare and health departments, rehabilitation centers, schools and day nurseries, and services for displaced persons and travelers

....

Casework in Action: Working with Individuals

Social workers must know how to help people change attitudes that prevent them from solving personal problems. Mrs. Preston, fifty-two years old, was a woman who had withdrawn from life and was unable to see any future for herself when the social worker from a family agency first came at the request of Mrs. Preston's daughter, with whom she lived.

Mrs. Preston's husband had died ten years before, and she had supported herself as a bookkeeper for a television repair shop. A serious operation had not only wiped out her savings but also left her too disabled to return to work, forcing her to move into her daughter's small apartment. The four rooms were jammed, mostly with Mrs. Preston's furniture, which she insisted on bringing with her. This had caused numerous and heated arguments with her daughter.

On the social worker's second visit, Mrs. Preston broke down and began to sob. "There's nothing ahead in life for me," she blurted out. "I can't work, and it's ten years before I can get Social Security. I wish I were dead."

The caseworker wisely ignored the remark and began to probe into Mrs. Preston's past, what she had done as a young girl, what hobbies she enjoyed, what skills, if any, she might have. She learned that Mrs. Preston liked to read and considered herself an extremely fast reader.

"Since you can't return to a regular job," the social worker said, "I wonder if we can think of some kind of work you can do here in your home." They discussed the matter at some length, but did not come to any decision, although Mrs. Preston seemed interested in the idea.

A few days later, the caseworker saw an advertisement for a local specialty shop seeking someone to read and clip newspaper articles. Immediately she thought it would be the perfect job for Mrs. Preston.

Mrs. Preston was enthusiastic about the idea but lacked courage to apply, for fear of being turned down. It took some time before her caseworker was able to convince her that this was perhaps part of her trouble and that she had to summon courage and apply herself. The next day, Mrs. Preston wrote a letter of application and was hired as soon as the manager of the store talked with her.

This clipping job led to two similar assignments for other merchants, and soon Mrs. Preston's income was equal to what she had been earning as a bookkeeper. The caseworker might have withdrawn at this point, satisfied that her job was done, but she felt there was something more she could do. Tactfully, she suggested to Mrs. Preston that either she might put some of her furniture in storage or offer to help pay for a larger apartment if her daughter would consent to move. The daughter was delighted at the suggestions, and, once the move had been completed, the social worker was able to close the case.

Sometimes the need is even more desperate. Joan Randolph of Hinsdale, Illinois, was the subject of numerous newspaper stories. She had fifteen children—including seven youngsters whose birth mother had died recently—and was expecting another when her husband suffered a severe heart attack. In addition, her car had broken down, and with the approach of cold weather, it was doubtful that her furnace would work. Nevertheless, she refused to be discouraged. The children pitched in while relatives and friends offered aid.

All families in trouble are not as resourceful, independent, or lucky as the Randolphs, however. Many have no place to go, except to the local relief agency, because they lack the means of helping themselves and have no friends or relatives to assist them.

A family like the Tates, who live in an impoverished area of a large city, is an example. Mr. Tate is disabled and cannot work. Mrs. Tate is frail and unable to hold a full-time job and care for their four children. Neighbors who are equally poor obviously cannot help. Such a family has no alternative but to look to the local welfare agency as the "neighborhood helping hand."

Casework in Action: Working with Groups

Some social workers work with groups of people in similar situations, instead of individuals. Although the scope and purpose of group work may vary among social service agencies or other institutions, such as schools or hospitals, the work usually includes one or more of the following activities:

- Directing camps and community centers
- Helping achieve better relations between different cultural and racial groups
- Organizing recreational programs for children, young people, adults, and the aged
- Planning group programs and working with patients in hospitals, institutions, and treatment centers to develop group living programs

In addition to this list of general activities, there are tasks and abilities specific to each social services area. The following description will give you a better idea of what to expect on the job in a range of settings, as well as a general description of the places in which you could expect to work.

Work with Communities

Agencies and institutions that offer career opportunities in the community include community welfare councils, housing bureaus, intergroup relations organizations, neighborhood centers, social action and planning bodies, and the United Way. Tasks you might be responsible for include:

- Helping the community plan for and operate necessary welfare services
- Coordinating existing community social services
- Encouraging and helping citizens become leaders in the social welfare field
- Raising funds and budgeting the monies needed for health and welfare agencies

Work in Social Research

Agencies and institutions that offer career opportunities in social research include national social service agencies, such as the Family Service Association of America; schools of social work; government agencies, such as the Bureau of Family Services or the Children's Bureau; and a few of the larger local agencies, such as the Community Service Society of New York. Tasks include:

- Obtaining, studying, and interpreting special data and information to determine the various social services needed in a community and to what extent they are being provided
- Devising better methods of conducting casework and providing other services
- Devising methods of measuring the cost of social services and their effectiveness

Work in Social Administration

All public and private social service and health agencies offer career opportunities in social administration. Tasks you might be responsible for include:

- Planning and directing the overall program of a social service or public welfare agency
- Employing, training, and supervising staff members
- Providing leadership in drawing up policies and operating procedures
- Administering financial affairs
- Cooperating with other public and private health and welfare agencies

Work in Teaching

Colleges, graduate schools of social work, medical schools, social agencies, and theological seminaries offer career opportunities in teaching for social workers. Your responsibilities might include:

- Teaching undergraduate college courses in social service
- Teaching in graduate schools of social service
- Giving field instruction in social agencies

On the Job with Group Social Workers

The following describes typical situations social workers who specialize in groups might encounter in their jobs.

- **A group of mothers**: In a low-income neighborhood, a few mothers meet regularly to discuss their children's behavior. A social worker joins the women to help them find solutions to their problems and initiate action that changes their own outlook on life as well as bringing improvements to the community.

- **Summer campers:** In a summer camp operated by a large social service agency, a worker is present to help the eight-, nine-, and ten-year-old girls make their first adjustment to living away from home and in a group. They must learn to do for themselves, to make decisions, and to work and play fairly with each other.
- **Senior Citizens' Club:** Some twenty retired men meet regularly at the local YMCA. Most of them have lost their wives and are lonely. A social worker concentrates on showing them how to build friendships with each other and channel their interests, skills, and energies into a variety of projects that will help improve the neighborhood and get them involved more deeply in the community.
- **Red Dragons:** Sixteen boys have banded together to form a gang. Soon they are fighting other youth gangs and tangling with police officers. A social worker undertakes the difficult task of gaining the boys' confidence in order to redirect their interests and activities away from violence and into more constructive projects or activities. The caseworker involves family members and community members in providing good role models for the boys.
- **Recovering patients:** In a mental hospital, a social worker meets with a group of patients who will soon be discharged. They need to talk out the worries and problems involved in the prospect of a return to the outside world. Some patients also require vocational guidance and help in solving personal problems.
- **In the Welfare Department:** A group of women who are receiving public assistance are invited to visit the welfare office on a regular basis. There, a social worker meets with them, affording them an opportunity to talk about themselves and their attitudes regarding public welfare and encouraging them to do something that will enable them to become independent.

The Benefits

Good opportunities for promotion exist in the social work field because of the shortage of qualified personnel. In addition, it is possible to move from one kind of practice to another without being forced to become a specialist. Women and men who marry and leave work to raise a family may expect a warm welcome upon returning.

Working conditions are good in the social work field. In most agencies, you can expect:

- Liberal annual paid vacations
- Generous sick leave
- Health and hospitalization insurance
- Retirement plans (in addition to Social Security coverage)
- Good personnel practices in handling employees

You will receive all these benefits in most vocations, but social work offers an added plus—the satisfaction of helping people. No matter what your job in social work, you are part of a team effort—your goal is to aid those in need or trouble.

The Outlook

The nation's social welfare needs are becoming so tremendous that many agencies cannot respond adequately to all who seek help. This is especially true in large cities where crime, unemployment, drugs, abuse, and other social ills make it impossible for countless victims to deal with their problems without outside help. Therefore, social workers and other professionals who work in these agencies, as well as members of the support staff, are essential to society's continuing response to these urgent and often desperate calls for help.

Unfortunately, there is not enough money available to provide the required army of caregivers, but because of turnover, expansion of services, and occasional unexpected additional financial support, career opportunities will continue to grow. There are thousands of local, county, and state social welfare agencies in the fifty states. In addition, there are more than a thousand national agencies.

If some aspect of this field interests you, read the books listed below and discuss your ideas with the personnel director of a nearby agency. Look in the Yellow Pages under "Social and Human Services" for a listing of all the organizations in your area. You may also consult the section on "Social Welfare Organizations" in *Gale's Encyclopedia of Associations* to learn about national and regional organizations.

....

For Further Information

Organizations

Council on Social Work Education
1725 Duke Street, Suite 500
Alexandria, VA 22314
www.cswe.org

National Association of Social Workers
750 First Street NE, Suite 700
Washington, DC 20002
www.naswdc.org

Social Work Access Network (SWAN)
www.sc.edu/swan
(A resource for international information for researchers.)

Canadian Association of Social Workers
383 Parkdale Avenue, Suite 402
Ottawa, ON K1Y 4R4
Canada
www.casw-acts.ca

Suggested Reading

Baxter, Neale J. *Opportunities in Counseling and Development Careers.* Chicago: VGM Career Books, 1997.
Garner, Geraldine O. *Careers in Social and Rehabilitation Services.* Chicago: VGM Career Books, 2001.
Wittenberg, Renee. *Opportunities in Social Work Careers.* Chicago: VGM Career Books, 2002.

CHAPTER TEN

Other Caregiving Careers

In this chapter, you will find suggestions for additional caregiving careers and pertinent organizations and associations to contact for information and further career exploration. Consider contacting someone at any one of these organizations and requesting an informational interview. You're likely to receive an enthusiastic response and find someone willing to talk at length about the necessary and important field of caregiving.

The Corporation for National and Community Service

The Corporation for National and Community Service is the principal agency in the federal government for administering volunteer service programs. The corporation's goal is to foster a culture of service, citizenship, and responsibility.

The agency administers and coordinates domestic volunteer programs sponsored by the federal government. These programs share a commitment to local initiatives that foster self-reliance and work to overcome poverty. It includes Volunteers in Service in America (VISTA), the Points of Light Foundation, the Foster Grandparent Program (FGP), the Retired Senior Volunteer Program (RSVP), the National Senior Volunteer Corps (also known at Senior Corps), and the various state offices of volunteerism.

For more information about this agency, general literature, and recruitment material, contact:

Corporation for National and Community Service
1201 New York Avenue NW
Washington, DC 20525
www.nationalservice.org

American Friends Service Committee

Founded in 1917 by the religious group known as the Quakers, or Friends, this organization has the overall purpose of relieving human suffering and carries out its objectives through three divisions: community relations, international, and peace education.

From a caregiving point of view, it manages numerous refugee and relief programs here and abroad and welcomes concerned men and women, regardless of their religious affiliations, to take part in its humanitarian programs. For information, write to:

American Friends Service Committee
1501 Cherry Street
Philadelphia, PA 19102
www.afsc.org

American Red Cross

Organized in 1881 by Clara Barton, the American Red Cross specializes in disaster relief and service to veterans and the armed forces and promotes safety and public health service programs.

Since the disaster of September 11, 2001, it would be hard to find an American not familiar with the Red Cross blood program, which collects and distributes blood, as well as with its lifesaving and other educational programs.

The American Red Cross also offers family casework service for members of the armed forces and their families, as well as for veterans and their families. Here, too, the caseworkers try to help soldiers and their families see their problems realistically and find solutions to their difficulties. Cases range from simple questions involving military regulations to unhappy and difficult family situations usually caused by the absence of the spouse or parent from the family group.

Although the organization relies on volunteers for many of its programs, numerous salaried positions are needed to operate this agency's many offices throughout the country. There are approximately three thousand chapters, of which fourteen hundred are staffed by volunteers; one or more paid staff members work in the remaining sixteen hundred chapters. Your local phone directory should list the address of the nearest office, which can tell you about its activities and career possibilities, or write to:

American Red Cross
National Headquarters
431 Eighteenth Street NW
Washington, DC 20006
www.redcross.org

Emergency Medical Technicians

In cases of automobile accident injuries, heart attacks, near drownings, childbirth, poisonings, and gunshot wounds, all of which demand urgent medical attention, Emergency Medical Technicians (EMTs) give immediate care and transport the injured or sick to medical facilities.

EMTs usually work in teams of two and drive specially equipped emergency vehicles; if necessary, they request additional help from fire, police, or utility personnel. They determine the nature and scope of the patient's injury then give appropriate emergency care following strict guidelines. The range of responsibilities is broad—they may open airways, restore breathing, control bleeding, treat for shock, administer oxygen, immobilize fractures, bandage wounds, assist in childbirth, manage emotionally disturbed patients, treat and help heart attack victims, give care to poison and burn victims, and treat patients with anti-shock trousers, which prevent blood pressure from falling too low. All of these emergency procedures can be performed by someone with EMT-Basic certification.

An EMT-Intermediate has more advanced training and may administer intravenous fluids and use defibrillators to give lifesaving shocks to a stopped heart. An EMT-Paramedic provides the most extensive prehospital care. In addition to all of the procedures already mentioned, he or she may administer drugs orally or intravenously, interpret EKGs, perform endotracheal intubations, and use monitors and other complex equipment.

In 2002, 870,000 Emergency Medical Service Providers (EMTs and First Responders) worked for private ambulance services, municipal fire, police, or rescue squad departments, and hospitals. Most are employed in metropolitan areas. Those who work in smaller cities and towns are often unpaid volunteers.

For basic training, 100 to 120 hours of classroom work plus 10 hours of internship in a hospital emergency room are required to be certified. Intermediate training varies from state to state but includes at least 35 to 55 hours of additional training, while the training program for paramedics requires between 750 and 2,000 hours. General information is available from:

National Association of Emergency Medical Technicians
408 Monroe Street
Clinton, MS 39056
www.naemt.org

. . . .

Foster Care

There is an urgent need in many communities for foster homes to take children who are in need of a home setting in which to live.

It can be a demanding responsibility, because it is a twenty-four-hour-a-day, seven-day-a-week undertaking. Eligibility varies from state to state, as do the rates of compensation. In New York City, all payments for foster care are untaxed by city, state, and federal governments. A foster-care household can have a maximum of six foster children or three of the family's children plus three foster-care children.

In Wisconsin, the monthly maintenance rate in 2002 for children from birth to four years old was approximately $300; for children age five to eleven years, $330; for ages twelve to fourteen years, $375; and for fifteen- to eighteen-year-olds, $390. These payments are to cover food, clothing, housing, basic transportation, personal care, and other expenses. Families caring for children with special needs may receive supplemental payments to cover additional costs.

For further information about foster care in your area, contact the local social services organization or the welfare department.

····················

Missionaries

"Wanted—Cyprus: personnel assistant; Pakistan: surgeon for six months and female physician for hospital; Kabul: leader for finance and administration group; Turkey: teacher."

These are typical openings for professionals who practice their professions and witness to their faiths, posted by a religious group active in sending workers to underdeveloped countries. In some countries, it is illegal to proselytize, and these specialists are admitted on this understanding. However, they feel that their work, sacrifices, and personal relationships are forceful ways of witnessing their faiths.

If you belong to an organized religious group, it may have an active and far-reaching missionary group, both in the United States and abroad. Contact the headquarters office for further information.

Homes for the Battered and Abused

You will find homes in many communities where men, women, and children in crisis can obtain temporary housing and sympathetic help. A typical shelter welcomes battered and abused people of every age, pregnant teens, young families, single homeless, the elderly, and foster children.

The mission of one such home is "to maintain a clean, comfortable, quiet environment for persons requiring temporary shelter, normally not to exceed two weeks. The emphasis is on shelter and privacy. We do not provide professional counseling or therapy services, but our staff is trained to facilitate referrals to appropriate caregivers."

Homelike facilities include private rooms with full bathroom, TV room, library, spacious dining area, communal kitchen, children's playroom, laundry room, big backyard and private garden.

Employment opportunities naturally depend on the size of a shelter. Apart from a director or directors (in the case of a married couple), there may be kitchen and housekeeping staffs. Since this can be a round-the-clock operation, it calls for a dedicated and sensitive staff capable of dealing with people who need an unusual amount and type of sympathetic and supportive assistance in an emergency. They are not there unless they are seriously threatened or abused, and job satisfaction must come from helping these individuals straighten out their lives. The director's job may not call for social service training, but it will require demonstrated ability to handle the demands of the position and knowledge of where to refer residents. These homes are listed in the Yellow Pages under the heading "Social and Human Services."

Nannies

Today, nannies are recognized as important caretakers for families needing a responsible person to take care of their children. A similar position and term is *au pair*, though typically the au pair is a young person exchanging housework for room and board and the opportunity to learn the local language.

While nannies and au pairs are both male and female, traditionally, women have dominated the field. However, there are opportunities for both men and women to work as nannies or home caretakers for children.

Responsibilities for nannies obviously vary from home to home. In one setting, a nanny may work only during the day when both parents are at work; in another, he or she may live in and be part of the household, helping with chores and sharing in many of the family activities.

For further information, contact:

International Nanny Association
900 Haddon Avenue, Suite 438
Collingswood, NJ 08108
www.nanny.org

Peace Corps

Have you wanted to travel and work in a foreign country? If so, you should investigate the possibility of joining the Peace Corps, a caregiving organization that offers tremendous opportunities in a wide range of fields.

Established in 1961 by executive order of President John F. Kennedy, the Peace Corps' purpose, according to organization literature, is "to promote world peace and friendship, to help other countries in meeting their needs for trained manpower, and to help promote understanding between the American people and other peoples served by the Peace Corps. The Corps' programming is designed to meet the basic needs of those living in the more than seventy poorest countries in which it operates."

After a nine- to fourteen-week training period to learn the local language, acquire technical skills necessary for the particular job, and deepen cross-cultural understanding, volunteers serve for two years, living among the people with whom they work. Volunteers are expected to become a part of the local community.

Volunteers are posted throughout Latin America, Africa, the Near East, Asia, the Pacific, and Eastern Europe. The work involves education, agriculture, health, small business development, urban development, and the environment. Projects are designed to match the skills of volunteers with the needs of the host countries.

The Peace Corps motto is "the toughest job you'll ever love!" With so many underdeveloped countries in upheaval, the Peace Corps has sometimes had to withdraw some of its programs until order is restored. When working for the Peace Corps, your living expenses are covered, and you receive a small stipend. If you want a salary commensurate with your involvement, look elsewhere. But, if you are looking for a way to help others while broadening your horizons, the Peace Corps could be your best bet.

For more information, contact:

Peace Corps
Office of Human Resources
1111 Twentieth Street NW, Room 2300
Washington, DC 20526
www.peacecorps.gov

Salvation Army

In 1878, Catherine and William Booth founded the Salvation Army in England. Essentially a military form of organization that adheres to the Protestant denomination and is in line with most Protestant evangelical groups, members wear uniforms and wage "warfare against evil." Purity of life and salvation are emphasized, but the sacraments of baptism and communion are not practiced.

The Salvation Army offers a wide range of social services. Like the American Red Cross, it provides disaster relief worldwide and operates numerous community centers, alcohol and drug rehabilitation centers, hospitals, centers for social work, community kitchens, and recreation facilities. The community center is the basic unit, administered by a commanding officer who directs the religious and social service activities. Officers receive college training, and the members, both men and women, are known as "soldiers." One does not need to be a member, however, to work with the organization.

A list from the Manhattan, New York, telephone book of Salvation Army branches gives you an idea of the organization's wide-ranging activities:

- Adult Rehabilitation Center for Men and Women
- Booth Memorial Medical Center (Hospital)
- Corps community centers
- Correctional services
- Disaster
- Foster home care
- Missing persons bureau
- Military services, Fort Hamilton
- Residences for men
- Residences for senior citizens
- Residences for women
- School for officers training
- Social services camping
- Thrift stores
- Truck pick-up service
- Women's treatment center

If there is no listing for the Salvation Army in your local phone directory, ask the public library reference librarian to help you find the address of the nearest office, or contact:

Salvation Army
P.O. Box 269
Alexandria, VA 22313
www.salvationarmyusa.org

. . . .

Volunteers of America

Similar to the Salvation Army, this group was founded in 1896 by members of the Booth family who left the army but retained the military form of organization with officers, titles, and uniforms. Although the agency has strong religious roots, it is nonsectarian and nondenominational. It operates more than a hundred kinds of services, including an extensive system of welfare activities such as services to prisoners, homes for the aged, maternity homes, day-care centers, and fresh-air camps in more than three hundred communities throughout the country. It currently employs more than ten thousand professionals and more than forty thousand volunteers. For information about volunteer and career opportunities, contact the national headquarters:

Volunteers of America
1600 Duke Street
Alexandria, VA 22314
www.volunteersofamerica.org

This book suggests many of the career opportunities for those interested in becoming a caregiver. The world has never needed the concern and dedication of caring men and women more than it does today. You have the opportunity to make something of yourself, do something important, and help the world become a better place.

. . . .

For Further Information

Suggested Reading

Eberts, Marjorie, and Margaret Gisler. *Careers for Good Samaritans and Other Humanitarian Types*. Chicago: VGM Career Books, 1998.

Suggested Reading

All of the following books are published by VGM Career Books, McGraw-Hill Companies, One Prudential Plaza, 130 East Randolph Street, Suite 900, Chicago, IL 60601.

Belikoff, Kathleen M. *Opportunities in Eye Care Careers*, 2003.

Frederickson, Keville. *Opportunities in Nursing Careers*, 2003.

Gable, Fred B. *Opportunities in Pharmacy Careers*, 2003.

Karni, Karen R. *Opportunities in Clinical Laboratory Science Careers*, 2002.

Kendall, Bonnie. *Opportunities in Dental Care Careers*, 2000.

Krumhansl, Bernice. *Opportunities in Physical Therapy Careers*, 1999.

Sacks, Terrence J. *Careers in Medicine*, 1996.

Sacks, Terrence J. *Opportunities in Physician Assistant Careers*, 2002.

Sherry, Clifford J. *Opportunities in Medical Imaging Careers*, 2000.

Snook, I. Donald Jr., and Leo D'Orazio. *Opportunities in Health and Medical Careers*, 1998.

Sugar-Webb, Jan. *Opportunities in Physician Careers*, 1999.

Super, Charles McAfee. *Opportunities in Psychology Careers*, 2000.

Swanson, Barbara. *Careers in Health Care*, 2000.

Tierney, Gillian. *Opportunities in Holistic Health Care Careers,*
1999.

Weeks, Zona R. *Opportunities in Occupational Therapy Careers,*
2000.

Williams, Ellen. *Opportunities in Gerontology and Aging Services
Careers,* 2002.

Career Statistics for Caregiving Jobs

T he statistics presented here are for the year 2000 (the latest
available at the time this book went to press) and were com-
piled by the U.S. Bureau of Labor Statistics. You can find current details on thousands of careers at your local library by asking
to see the *Occupational Outlook Handbook*. These statistics are
also easy to locate on the Web by visiting www.bls.gov/oco.

The numbers following the job titles indicate the total number
of workers in that field. The capital letters referring to the job outlook are defined below:

A. Will grow much faster than the average
B. Will grow faster than the average
C. Will grow about as fast as the average
D. Will grow more slowly than the average
E. Will show little change—neither increase nor decrease

Average or median annual earnings are included wherever
available, and in a few instances these are expressed in terms of
hourly, weekly, or monthly amounts.

The final numeral refers to the minimum education required.
In many cases, employers will look for more than the minimum,
and in some cases, whole industries are moving toward requiring
more education in order to hire people who have achieved a
certificate or degree in the field. Be sure to look at the "training"

section for different careers listed in the *Occupational Outlook Handbook* for details on the amount of education typically required. Following are the education-level codes used in this appendix.

1. High school diploma
2. High school plus one year in a vocational-technical school
3. High school plus two years in a vocational-technical school
4. Four years college
5. Undergraduate degree plus one year graduate school
6. Undergraduate degree plus six to nine years graduate school according to program selected

	Number Empl.	Job Outlook	Median Earnings	Minimum Education
Administrative Services Manager	362,000	C	$40,000	1
Billing Clerk	506,000	D	$12.17/hr	1
Bookkeeping, Accounting, and Auditing Clerk	2 million	E	$12.34/hr	1
Building Worker/ Janitor	4.2 million	C	$17,180	1
Cardiovascular Technologist and Technician	39,000	B	$33,000	2
Chef, Cook, and Other Food Preparation Workers	3.1 million	C	$7.38–$8.22/hr	1
Child-Care Worker	1.2 million	C	$7.43/hr	1
Chiropractor	50,000	B	$81,500	6
Clinical Laboratory Technologist and Technician	295,000	C	$40,840	4
Dental Assistant	247,000	A	$12.49/hr	1
Dental Hygienist	147,000	A	$24.68/hr	3
Dentist	152,000	D	$129,030	6
Dietitian	49,000	C	$38,450	4
Emergency Medical and Paramedic	172,000	B	$22,460	3
General Office Clerk	2.7 million	C	$21,130	1
Health Services Manager	250,000	A	$56,370	4

	Number Empl.	Job Outlook	Median Earnings	Minimum Education
Homemaker/Home Health Aide	615,000	A	$8.89/hr	1
Information and Record Clerk	5.1 million	B	$20,400	1
Personal Home Care Aide	414,000	A	$7.50/hr	1
Licensed Practical Nurse (LPN)	700,000	C	$29,440	2
Mail Clerk	188,000	C	not available	1
Maintenance Mechanic	1.1 million	B	$9.37/hr	1
Maintenance Worker and Groundskeeper	1.1 million	B	$12/hr	1
Medical Assistant	181,000	A	$15,059	1
Medical Records and Health Information Technician	76,000	A	$11.30/hr	3
Medical Transcriptionist	102,000	B	$12.15/hr	2
Nuclear Medicine Technologist	18,000	B	$44,130	2
Nursing Aide	1.4 million	A	$8.89/hr	1
Nutritionist, see *Dietitian*				
Occupational Therapist	78,000	A	$49,450	4
Occupational Therapy Assistant and Aide	25,000	A	$34,000 Assistant $20,710 Aide	1 1
Optometrist	31,000	C	$82,860	6
Payroll and Timekeeping Clerk	201,000	E	$13.07/hr	1
Pharmacist	217,000	B	$70,950	4

	Number Empl.	Job Outlook	Median Earnings	Minimum Education
Physical and Corrective Therapy Assistant and Aide	80,000	A	$33,870	1
Physical Therapist	132,000	A	$54,810	4
Physician Assistant	58,000	A	$61,910	3
Physician/Surgeon	598,000	C	$160,000	6
Podiatrist	18,000	B	$107,560	6
Public Relations Specialist	137,000	A	$39,580	4
Radiologic Technologist	167,000	B	$30,220	3
Receptionist	1.1 million	B	$20,040	1
Recreational Therapist	29,000	D	$28,650	4
Registered Nurse	2.2 million	B	$37,680	3
Respiratory Therapist	110,000	B	$37,680	3
Secretary/ Administrative Assistant	3.9 million	D	$31,090	1
Social Services Assistant	271,000	A	$22,330	1
Social Worker	468,000	B	$31,470	5
Speech/Language Pathologist/Audiologist	101,000	A	$46,640	5
Surgical Technologist	71,000	B	$29,020	3
Telephone Operator/ Communications Equipment Operator	339,000	D	$9.71/hr	1

About the Author

A drian Paradis was born in Brooklyn, New York, and graduated from Dartmouth College and Columbia University's School of Library Service. As a writer, businessman, vocational specialist, and researcher, he has been published widely, with more than fifty titles to his credit. He has covered subjects ranging from banking to biographies of contemporary businesspeople and scientists; from public relations to religion; from vocational guidance to reference works; and from economics to law. In addition, he has worked on reports and special studies in his capacity as a corporate executive.

Adrian spent more than twenty years as an officer of a major national corporation handling corporate matters, economic analysis, stockholder relations, corporate philanthropic contributions, and security and general administrative responsibilities. He lives in Sugar Hill, New Hampshire, and is retired.